LIBRARIES AND THE SUBSTANCE ABUSE CRISIS

ALA Editions purchases fund advocacy, awareness,
and accreditation programs for library professionals worldwide.

LIBRARIES AND THE SUBSTANCE ABUSE CRISIS

Supporting Your Community

CINDY GROVE

ALA Editions
CHICAGO 2020

CINDY GROVE is the director of a public library in New England. She has worked in libraries for over sixteen years and also has five years' experience working with various social service agencies. Throughout her life she has worked with people with substance use disorders and their loved ones. She has also appeared as a panelist for several webinars that focus on substance use disorders and mental health.

© 2020 by the American Library Association

Extensive effort has gone into ensuring the reliability of the information in this book; however, the publisher makes no warranty, express or implied, with respect to the material contained herein.

ISBN: 978-0-8389-4739-5

Library of Congress Control Number: 2020000790

Cover design by Kim Thornton. Cover images © Adobe Stock.

Text design in the Chaparral, Gotham, and Bell Gothic typefaces.

♾ This paper meets the requirements of ANSI/NISO Z39.48-1992 (Permanence of Paper).

Printed in the United States of America

24 23 22 21 20   5 4 3 2 1

I dedicate this book to the
librarians who are willing to fight.

Contents

Preface ix
Acknowledgments xiii
Introduction: We Have a Crisis xv

1 |	**The Library's Role in the Fight against Addiction**	1
2 |	**Understanding Addiction**	7
3 |	**People in Distress**	13
4 |	**Behavior and Stigma**	21
5 |	**Library Safety and Security**	25
6 |	**Library Policies**	31
7 |	**Library Services**	39
8 |	**Library Outreach and Marketing**	51
9 |	**Staff Training**	57
	Conclusion: Being Part of the Solution 63	

APPENDIXES

A *Observable Signs of Common Drugs* 65

B *Further Reading and Viewing* 91

Index 103

Preface

LIKE SO MANY, I HAVE A CHILDHOOD FILLED WITH MANY WONderful and heart-warming memories, and also some traumatic life-changing events. For most of my childhood I grew up in a low-income government housing development in Massachusetts. I was surrounded by people living in distress in my own home and in most of the homes around us. The people living in this community were (and still are) heavily impacted by violence, addiction, poverty, and neglect. The housing project area was surrounded by woods (which were not safe for children) and a major highway, which isolated the community. One resource I did have access to was the public library, because they had a bookmobile. The bookmobile would visit my neighborhood every other week. If it were not for the bookmobile, my access to information and recreational reading would have been greatly restricted. The resources I could access from that bookmobile had an enormous impact on my success in life; they enabled me to become a lifelong learner, and they provided materials that helped me experience the world outside of my own personal horizons.

During my childhood and teen years, I didn't understand the influence that drugs and alcohol had on my own family. While I was growing up, the emotions displayed in my family were intense, and I often felt like I was walking on eggshells. I never knew if those around me would be happy, furious, or deeply depressed. I never understood that the conditions I was living in were not normal. It was not until my 50-year-old stepfather died and I was told that he had struggled with addiction that I fully understood the challenges my family had been facing. I was shocked by this information, but then I was able to look back and realize all the signs I had missed growing up. The loss of my stepfather's life opened my eyes not only to his own substance use disorder, but to those of other family members and friends who have been part of my life.

My personal struggles and concern for those around me inspired me to pursue a degree in psychology. Armed with this degree, I worked for various social service agencies. I had the opportunity to work with many different populations, including those struggling with developmental disabilities, young adults and children removed from their families by the state, seniors trying to maintain a safe living environment at home, and people calling in to a crisis intervention hotline. I loved working in the field of psychology and having the opportunity to make a difference in people's lives, but I was often overwhelmed by the level of need and the limited resources available. I was frustrated by the limitations often put in place by the organizations I worked for, as well as by the limitations of insurance coverage.

In 2005, I was inspired by my best friend to embrace my lifelong love of libraries and join the profession. I enrolled in the GLIS program at Simmons University in Boston, and my first library position involved working ten hours a week in the children's and circulation departments of a small public library. I immediately knew that I had made the right career decision, and since then I have had the honor to work with several wonderful public libraries, first as a reference librarian and now as a library director. I love assisting the public with whatever goals or needs they have at the various stages of their lives. The opportunity to transform someone's life is an honor that I have always been grateful for. Sometimes, when I help someone research a sensitive topic and see them walk away with the information they need, that moment can be so powerful and inspirational for me. I have also been thankful for the patrons who have shared those occasions when a small moment (such as attaching a resume to an e-mail or finding a family member's obituary) had a profound impact on their lives. I love welcoming each patron every day and enjoying whatever journey they choose to take me on.

In 2013 I began working as the head of reference services at the Tewksbury Public Library in Massachusetts. Tewksbury is a blue-collar town of about 28,000 residents. The Tewksbury Public Library is located next to the grounds of the Tewksbury State Hospital. In addition to the hospital, there are several detox and rehabilitation facilities on the same property. At that time the library did not have a formal strategic plan, so I began reviewing how my department was serving the community and which groups we were serving well, and which groups were underserved.

As I began to familiarize myself with the library and the community, I noticed the high number of behavior-related incidents in the library that required direction or support. Some of the library's patrons had wild mood swings—ranging from extremely positive to very aggressive—and they engaged in frequent pacing and showed signs of sweating and exhaustion. The library had a no-sleeping policy, and I found myself waking people up multiple times a day. I was not sure why so many people were exhibiting such odd behaviors, and I wondered what the cause could be. I found myself spending more time trying to correct patrons' behaviors than doing anything else during my workday at the library. I realized then that I needed to focus on the source of these behavior issues and try to find a solution, so that the library could be more welcoming and I could provide services more effectively to everyone.

I first reached out to the Tewksbury community services officer, Jennie Welch. I told her of my observations based on documented incident reports. She confirmed that the behaviors were consistent with people using and detoxing from substances. She told me about the increasing problems surrounding opiate use in the community and what steps the police department was taking to assist those with a substance use disorder and their families. She also told me about several local organizations that were trying to provide support to drug users and their families. I was amazed by the organizations that were in my library's area and the connections the police department had with those organizations. I instantly wanted the library to become part of the solution. The patrons were already visiting the library, and I wanted to find a way to make their visits an opportunity to provide them with support.

I started with a permanent display located away from the reference desk that included books, information about local services, handouts on addiction from other organizations, and a resource guide I had created that included print and online resources available at the library as well as a list of local organizations. I also kept information in a subject file for staff working at the desk. As I reached out to the different organizations, I would also ask them if they would be willing to speak at the library. These events would often have a mix of people interested in learning about addiction, those supporting someone with an addiction, and those with an addiction. At these events, Officer Welch was able to offer access to recovery services immediately should anyone express an interest in them.

Around this time, a nearby public library invited local librarians to attend a presentation by Warren Graham, the author of *The Black Belt Librarian*. Graham was discussing patron behavior in the library and how to create as welcoming and safe a space as possible. He spoke about ways to prevent and handle inappropriate behavior in a clear and simple fashion. Immediately following his presentation, the staff at our library worked together to create a patron behavior policy that told patrons about expected behavior and what to expect if their behavior was inappropriate. With a solid policy to back us up, we had the authority we needed not only to redirect the behavior safely, but to also to reach out and offer assistance to those patrons. As the larger behavioral issues declined, we could quickly address smaller issues, and this led to a much more welcoming library for all.

Over time, word spread that I was open to discussing addiction and could offer support. Patrons would come to me for information and to access resources they needed for themselves or others. What was previously a huge stress on the library had become a strength.

I have since become the director of a public library, where I have been able to listen to a new community and use my previous experiences to create a library that is welcoming and responsive to all community needs.

It is my hope that by sharing my experiences and research, you will feel encouraged and supported to reach out to people in your community who are dealing with addiction. I hope this book will change your life the way mine has changed, from being overwhelmed, stressed, and at times scared to feeling empowered, energized, and ready to fight. It only takes one person to shift the balance in a library from stress to strength. When others feel your strength and confidence, they will follow and pitch in. Taking the first steps is often the scariest part, and my goal in this book is to make each of your steps ones you can take with confidence.

Acknowledgments

I WOULD LIKE TO THANK ALL THE PATRONS WHO HAVE TRUSTED me with their reference questions and given me the opportunity to learn and grow with them. To Diane Giarrusso, the director of the Tewksbury Public Library, thank you for giving me the freedom to try and for empowering me to become the director I am today. To the Tewksbury community services officer, Jennie Welch, you have been a joy to work with and collaborate with on this topic. Jennie, your love and support for the town of Tewksbury is such a gift. To Lee Mansfield, the love of my life and my best friend, thank you for your never-ending support and understanding. You always encourage me to believe in myself, be my best self, and reach for the stars. To my mother, Mona, who is one of the strongest women I know and an inspiration. To my brother, Wayne, you gave me something to fight for. I have been so lucky to be your big sister, and I love you. To my editor, Jamie Santoro, thank you for all your positive reinforcement and for making this book possible. I could not have done it without you.

Introduction

WE HAVE A CRISIS

DRUG OVERDOSE DEATHS CONTINUE TO INCREASE IN THE United States. According to the CDC, from 1999 to 2017, more than 702,000 people died from a drug overdose (Centers for Disease Control and Prevention 2019). In some communities, people may be struggling with alcohol addiction, while others may be dealing with meth or LSD. In a growing number of communities, however, the drug of most concern is opioids. Government and health professionals are attempting to regulate the distribution and use of these substances, but in the meantime, people are dying from overdoses at staggering rates.

People struggling with addiction visit libraries and use their resources for support. Libraries have a responsibility to help and protect the people in their space. Understanding the signs of overdose, what to do when someone does overdose, and how to process the results (both managerially and emotionally) is a first step toward being prepared. Overdoses can and will happen, so being prepared is truly our only option. Libraries have the opportunity to be part of the recovery process for our patrons, our communities, and the nation.

REFERENCE

Centers for Disease Control and Prevention. 2019. "Opioid Overdose." www.cdc.gov/drugoverdose/index.html.

1
The Library's Role in the Fight against Addiction

PUBLIC LIBRARIES ARE AND SHOULD BE A REFLECTION OF THE communities they serve. Libraries are a community space where everyone is welcome, so they are used widely by patrons who are in a difficult period of life. With the growth of drug addiction in the nation, many libraries have seen an increase of usage by people with substance use disorders and the people (friends, family, and coworkers) caring for them. Just like every other patron, patrons in distress are looking for comfort, security, information, and relaxation. It is often distressing to read discussions about the library's role in working with people struggling with addiction, because these are primarily about the impact that people with substance use disorders have on libraries, rather than on how library resources can help people who have substance use disorders. In a recent webinar, one librarian mentioned that their library only became aware of the issue of substance use addiction in their community after there was a fatal overdose at the library (WebJunction and PLA 2017). It is critical that libraries become aware of the opioid crisis and prepare for potential emergencies in their facilities.

The American Library Association's statement on the "Core Values of Librarianship" demonstrates its understanding of social responsibility. It states:

> The broad social responsibilities of the American Library Association are defined in terms of the contribution that librarianship can make in ameliorating or solving the critical problems of society; support for efforts to help inform and educate the people of the United States on these problems and to encourage them to examine the many views on and the facts regarding each problem; and the willingness of ALA to take a position on current critical issues, with the relationship to libraries and library service set forth in the position statement. (American Library Association 2004)

Libraries need to listen and respond to their communities in both large and small ways. We buy the latest James Patterson and Nora Roberts novels because those are what our patrons request, and we see many libraries expanding their e-content collections and programming because that is what their communities need. Similarly, recovery from substance use disorders is a community need that libraries should address. Ignoring the issue of drug addiction, or treating it merely as a disturbance in the library, are policies that fall short of our mission as public libraries, and fail to serve the best interests of our communities.

The library is a welcoming space that is warm when the weather is cold and cool when the weather is hot. We offer comfortable seating, access to technology, and privacy in clean bathrooms. Libraries do not require membership or check patrons' identification at the door. People can visit the library for just a few minutes or all day, from opening to close. Libraries are welcome to *everyone*. When patrons struggling with addiction visit the library, it is a chance for the community and library to provide a space, resources, and support for them to transform their lives. It is the library's responsibility to fight for the success of its community, and as part of that to fight against addiction.

I understand all too well that people struggling with addiction can bring disruptive behaviors into the library. People with a substance use disorder are desperate for drugs and may sell, buy, and use drugs in the library. The use and distribution of drugs is a serious concern because of the risk of overdose in the library, the safety of other visitors and staff, and the fact that the activity is illegal. Overdoses in the library have thrust library staff into a tough place where they wonder whether they should carry naloxone and get trained on how to provide lifesaving first aid. When someone does overdose, librarians are forced to make quick decisions which may save that person's life. Most professionals who decided to become a librarian never imagined themselves being placed in this position. Most of us became librarians for our love of reading, intellectual freedom, access to information, and public service.

Yet, working with patrons in crisis is part of the public service we provide to the communities we serve. We help the patron who wants to research cancer after receiving a diagnosis from their doctor. We support the patron who lost their job and is looking to write a resume. We support the patron from a foreign country who wants to learn to speak and read English. We support the child struggling to find a fiction genre that they will love for the rest of their life. We support the young adult who is acting out and trying to discover their future. Why would we not support someone struggling with addiction and help them stay alive and recover?

Library services can have a positive impact on a person's recovery and a family's ability to care for someone struggling with addiction. Being a welcoming space for people struggling with addiction and for their support system will demonstrate public concern and provide opportunities for recovery and growth. In addition to being a welcoming space, libraries can also offer support through programs, materials, resource guides, and community outreach.

As you begin targeting your library's services and resources to assist people with a substance use disorder, you should keep your community and stakeholders aware of your library's concerns, ideas, goals, and objectives. Keep them informed regarding your successes and setbacks. Ongoing communication will be a critical step because you want your community to know what you're trying to do, so that they might become involved and participate in your program offerings, and so that they're not taken by surprise should the problems already visible in your library become more visible in the wider community.

One of the significant hurdles surrounding the opioid crisis is the shame of addiction. People don't want to admit they have a problem, that they know someone who has a problem, or that there is a problem in their community. Librarians must combat the social stigma that is attached to people with substance use disorders by informing the public what is happening at their library and what the library is doing about it. It is up to the library to shape the message that it communicates to others.

If your library starts to talk about addiction in a way that is supportive, people will hear your message and reach out to you for help. Your staff and the board may also hear from those who don't believe there is an issue in the community and are fearful that the library will be less welcoming if it offers services to people who are struggling with addiction. This is where having honest discussions with local public safety officials and substance use support agencies can help generate the community awareness that is needed to support your library's actions. It is also helpful to review your library's mission statement and the ALA's various statements and policies. Examining these documents will let you know if you are on the right path for your library.

The library can play a major role in preventing substance addiction. Connecting people with information and resources can prevent someone from trying drugs, and an awareness of the risks associated with prescription drug misuse can make a significant difference in that person's life. Libraries may have opportunities to partner with schools to offer drug prevention programs and to encourage and support drug awareness and prevention. There has been an increase in the number of compelling fiction and nonfiction books for adults, young adults, and children that discuss addiction and recovery, so displaying these books in your library can help educate everyone about the risks associated with drug use. (See appendix B at the end of this book for a list of helpful titles.)

The library can also serve as a welcoming resource for people who are actively using drugs. This could be by simply making sure that if they do need medical attention, someone in the library will notice this and seek help. In addition, the library can offer a way for people to seek the resources they need in the library on their own (through a display or resource guide), or by approaching a librarian or speaking to someone at a library program. These ways of reaching out to people using drugs can transform and possibly save someone's life.

There is not enough support in our communities for people seeking recovery. There are so many stories of people who want to get treatment but are unable to find an available bed, or who have to wait on seemingly endless lists for a treatment center to find space for them. And even when people do get treatment, it may not be sufficient, since a twenty-eight-day rehabilitation process is often not enough. People need additional support in order to make their recovery a success.

For people in recovery, visiting the library can be an early step for them in rebuilding their lives. They might visit the library because they are looking for additional recovery services; or a new job; or simply for books and movies that might help take their minds off their situation, or for stories of inspiration to encourage them to stay sober. For many it may be the first time they have visited a library, but they quickly discover the wide variety of services and resources the library offers. For some, the library's computer equipment may be the only way they can reach out to family and friends and update them on where they are and how they are doing. At a lecture I attended with David Sheff, the author of *Beautiful Boy: A Father's Journey through His Son's Addiction*, he stated that his son's use of public library computers to send e-mails was how he knew where his son was and that he was alive.

The family and friends of people with a substance use disorder are another group that the library can have a role in serving. They might come in with a recent crisis, such as an overdose or an act of violence or theft by their loved one. They might not know where their loved one is and if they are safe. Materials, resource guides, programs, and understanding staff can assist these people to help not only their loved one, but also themselves.

People in our communities are struggling and dying. In order to win the fight against addiction and to support those in recovery, we have to become active on every level. Addiction is an individual problem, and those struggling with addiction and recovery need individual attention and support. Addiction is a family problem, and the family systems of those with addiction and in recovery all need support. Addiction is a community problem, and the community needs to come together and provide services and support for its members. Addiction is a state problem, and we all need support organizations, laws, and guidance to respond in a way that supports recovery. Addiction is a national problem that needs government oversight, regulations, and laws to prevent, protect, and support everyone.

Libraries can make small changes that cumulatively have a large and long-lasting impact on the people in their communities. The impact you have will not go unnoticed, and patrons who are aware of the substance abuse epidemic will see the library as being part of the solution. The public will see a library listening to its community and doing what it can to support it.

REFERENCES

American Library Association. 2004. "Core Values of Librarianship." June 29. www.ala.org/advocacy/intfreedom/corevalues.

WebJunction and PLA. 2017. "Opioid Crisis Town Hall: Library Needs and Responses." www.webjunction.org/events/webjunction/opioid-crisis-town-hall.html.

2

Understanding Addiction

ACCORDING TO THE U.S. NATIONAL LIBRARY OF MEDICINE, addiction occurs when a person's use of alcohol or a drug leads to health issues or problems at work, school, or home. Taking a broad view, health issues may include physical, mental, and even spiritual health.

There are many conflicting and interesting theories of addiction that have been and continue to be proposed. Going to the PubMed website and looking at the varying types of research being done on the topic of addiction is overwhelming and inspiring. Ongoing studies provide great information on what people with a substance use disorder and their families are going through, as well as the new trends in recovery and addiction prevention. Many of the studies available are unable to discuss one theory without mentioning another, and so we will examine the arguments as a whole. Keeping up-to-date on current trends and theories of addiction is a good way to keep connected to the subject and stay informed on changes in viewpoints that might affect your patrons.

Causes of Addiction

It is helpful to think about the biological, social, psychological, and other causes of addiction as you work with individuals and communities.

Psychological Causes

There are many psychological reasons why someone might use drugs, and all addictive drugs are taken because of some influence they have on our brain. These drugs interfere with how our brains work and can mimic, activate, or block neurotransmitters (chemical messengers that transmit signals between neurons). Some commonly used drugs increase the amount of the transmitter dopamine in the brain. Dopamine regulates what is perceived as pleasure and happiness. People may start to use drugs in order to lower their stress level; manage anxiety, depression, or some other emotional disorder; to experience a euphoria or "high"; to detach from reality; or simply to alleviate boredom.

Social Causes

Being exposed to substance use in the family or around friends can undoubtedly affect how we feel about substance use by others and ourselves. Growing up in a family where drug use is present may increase the likelihood that a young person will start to use drugs because it is what they see and experience as normal behavior, or because they have relatively easy access to drugs. Several studies demonstrate that children who grow up in situations where family members use drugs are more likely to use drugs themselves when they get older.

Physiological Causes

Many physiological theories focus on the genetic causes of addiction. In recent years, with the opioid crisis gaining national attention, more funding has been provided for this research, which involves researchers trying to determine which genes are responsible for a person being predisposed to addiction.

Whether or not addiction is a disease has been a long-standing debate. The National Institute on Drug Abuse believes that addiction is in fact a disease. Addiction can be compared to some cancers and diabetes because science has found that there are both genetic and lifestyle choices that determine if a person becomes ill. When identified as a disease, addiction also offers more opportunity for recovery. Detoxing and recovery will often require medical supervision. If part of treatment is medically based, then this shows that at least part of the cause of addiction is also medically based. Moreover, by designating addiction as a disease, this provides more opportunity for treatment that is covered by medical insurance.

There is a long-held belief in our country that addiction is a sign of personal weakness or low morality. The shame engendered by this attitude has made the opioid crisis a silent epidemic where people die every day, but we still don't want to talk about it or acknowledge it. Meeting and talking with people in recovery and reading the memoirs of people who struggled with addiction showed me that addiction is a disease and not a personal choice, and that my only option is to believe in and advocate for anyone who wants to recover from an addiction.

Addiction and the Opioid Crisis

Many articles attribute the current opioid crisis to the overprescribing of pain medication by doctors. In this instance, a patient would go in with a pain complaint, such as a sprained ankle or injured back, and then be prescribed an opioid painkiller such as OxyContin. For some individuals, taking just one of these pills triggers an addictive response. Medical researchers are still trying to understand why some people respond with addictive behaviors while others can take the medications without concern, but at this point, there is no way of knowing how someone will respond to a prescription drug until they take it.

Multiple government agencies have begun work on trying to reduce the use of opioid medications as prescribed and refilled by physicians in order to combat the opioid crisis. In 2014, the U.S. Drug Enforcement Administration (DEA) moved opioids into a more restrictive class of drugs (DEA 2014). Despite this change, a 2018 study published in the *Journal of the American Medical Association* showed an immediate and significant increase in the number of opioids prescribed after the reclassification (Habbouche et al. 2018). In 2016 the Centers for Disease Control (CDC) issued guidelines for physicians prescribing opioids for chronic pain (Dowell, Haegerich, and Chou 2016), and in 2018 it published a guide for implementing the guidelines (CDC 2018). The Food and Drug Administration (FDA) has responded to these guidelines by awarding a contract to the National Academies of Sciences, Engineering, and Medicine to develop evidence-based guidelines for prescribing opioids; the FDA is hoping to build on the initial steps in developing federal guidelines taken by the CDC (FDA 2018). In 2018, the DEA proposed a manufacturing reduction of opioid medications as part of the government's plan to reduce opioid prescription rates by one-third in three years (United States Department of Justice 2018).

Despite the efforts of these government agencies to restrict opioid use, in November 2018 the FDA approved the use of a new opioid, Dsuvia, which is 1,000 times stronger than morphine and ten times stronger than fentanyl. The drug's use will be limited to settings in health care institutions, but there are concerns that the drug will soon become part of and worsen the opioid crisis (May 2018). Dsuvia is available in a tablet form that is meant to dissolve under the tongue. It was developed to assist in acute pain management when intravenous drugs and pills would be less effective, and the new drug also acts more quickly to address pain (such as in active combat situations) (Jackson 2018). The potential for abuse of this powerful drug in the midst of the opioid crisis is a serious concern, however.

Identifying Addiction

Addiction is a destructive force in the lives of both those who are using drugs and those around them. The substance a person is addicted to becomes the most important thing in their life. Work, family, friends, money, and any other interests all become secondary to obtaining the drug. A person's dependence rests not only on the need to maintain the "high" or comfort the drug provides, but on the even greater need to avoid the effects of withdrawal from the drug.

It is important to familiarize yourself with some of the most commonly abused substances and their observable effects so that when you do meet someone in the library and notice behaviors or symptoms of concern, you will be able to better understand the situation and the needs of the person you are observing. (See appendix A for a list of these substances and their observable effects.) Being aware of the signs of drug use may help you prevent a possible overdose and save someone's life. It is also critical to listen to your patrons and even attend a local meeting of those struggling with addiction, or the family and friends of those who are struggling. The more you listen, the better you will be able to identify, understand, and support those with a substance use disorder.

REFERENCES

CDC Centers for Disease Control and Prevention. 2018. "Quality Improvement and Care Coordination: Implementing the CDC Guideline for Prescribing Opioids for Chronic Pain." National Center for Injury Prevention and Control, Division of Unintentional Injury Prevention. www.cdc.gov/drugoverdose/pdf/prescribing/CDC-DUIP-QualityImprovementAndCareCoordination-508.pdf.

DEA Drug Enforcement Administration. 2014. "DEA to Publish Final Rule Rescheduling Hydrocodone Combination Products." www.dea.gov/press-releases/2014/08/21/dea-publish-final-rule-rescheduling-hydrocodone-combination-products.

Dowell, D., T. M. Haegerich, and R. Chou. 2016. "CDC Guidelines for Prescribing Opioids for Chronic Pain—United States, 2016." MMWR Recomm Rep 65, No. RR-1 (March): 1–49. http://dx.doi.org/10.15585/mmwr.rr6501e1.

FDA Federal Drug Administration. 2018. "Statement by FDA Commissioner Scott Gottlieb, M.D., on New Steps to Advance the Development of Evidence-Based, Indication-Specific Guidelines to Help Guide Appropriate Prescribing of Opioid Analgesics." August 22. www.fda.gov/newsevents/newsroom/pressannouncements/ucm617908.htm.

Habbouche, J., J. Lee, R. Steiger, et al. 2018. "Association of Hydrocodone Schedule Change with Opioid Prescriptions Following Surgery." JAMA Surgery 153, no. 12 (December): 1111–19. https://jamanetwork.com/journals/jamasurgery/article-abstract/2696622.

Jackson, Anna. 2018. "What Is Dsuvia? What You Should Know about the New Opioid Drug That's 10 Times Stronger Than Fentanyl." ABC News, October 31. https://abcnews.go.com/Health/dsuvia-opioid-painkiller/story?id=58875487.

May, Ashley. 2018. "FDA Approves Opioid Painkiller 1,000 Times Stronger Than Morphine." USA Today Network, November 5. www.usatoday.com/story/news/nation-now/2018/11/05/fda-approves-opioid-painkiller-stronger-than-morphine-fentanyl/1889389002/.

U.S. Department of Justice. 2018. "Justice Department, DEA Propose Significant Opioid Manufacturing Reduction in 2019." www.justice.gov/opa/pr/justice-department-dea-propose-significant-opioid-manufacturing-reduction-2019.

3

People in Distress

THERE ARE MANY PEOPLE LIVING IN DISTRESS IN OUR COMMUnities. A person in distress is someone who is struggling in their personal life and needs additional services and support from family, friends, the community, and the library. A patron in distress may be working through something seemingly small like a failing grade on a math test, or something significant like bankruptcy, divorce, or a serious illness. When the person is unable to cope with the issue and move beyond it, he or she is in distress. Similarly, people with a substance use disorder may be high-functioning and you may never know that they are using drugs, or they may be hitting a real low point and are desperate for any services the library can offer. Their addiction may also be compounded by additional issues such as joblessness, mental health problems, or even homelessness. Additionally, the family members of those with a substance use disorder may also be experiencing deep distress. No one chooses to become addicted; it is not something that feels good or is rewarding. When people understand that addiction is an illness, it encourages compassion, empathy, and a greater desire to support those who are struggling. It is through compassion and connection that our libraries can become the welcoming, resourceful, and community-focused organizations that they all strive to be.

Mental Health Disorders and Addiction

Drug use and mental health problems are not always separate issues for people. A 2017 National Survey on Drug Use and Health reported that out of the 18.7 million adults with a substance use disorder, 3.1 million also had a serious mental health disorder (Substance Abuse and Mental Health Services Administration 2018). In talking with several mental health professionals and those working in rehabilitation facilities, I learned that the number of people suffering from a mental health disorder is higher than reported and that the use of drugs is one way that these people self-medicate. If someone has both a mental health disorder and a substance use disorder, they are identified as having a co-occurring disorder. Co-occurring disorders were previously referred to as a dual diagnosis or dual disorder. According to an article in *Psychology Today*, "Approximately 7.9 million adults in the United States had co-occurring disorders in 2014" (*Psychology Today* 2018).

Libraries have an important role to play in the well-being of the people in our communities, and especially in support of their mental health. We traditionally do this by offering materials and services that support lifelong learning and recreation, but we can do more than that. Many people will struggle with a mental health problem (like depression or anxiety) at some point in their lives, and libraries can be part of the recovery process. Librarians can support people with a mental health issue and/or addiction by understanding that a person's mental health is an important part of who they are, but a mental health problem should not be used to define them. Librarians should educate themselves on some common forms of mental disorders and work to support those patrons as they would other patrons with a physical illness.

A library can provide a welcoming space by treating everyone with respect and offering resources to anyone in a crisis. We can make the library a comfortable place for people to ask questions and inquire about the mental health resources that are available for themselves or a loved one. When libraries demonstrate that all are welcome by not shaming, ignoring, or banning people who are struggling with a mental illness, it will enable librarians to step into a role of support.

Homelessness and Addiction

Homelessness is not always related to addiction, but there is often a connection between them. Someone struggling with addiction may lose everything and become homeless; they may be forced to leave their home because of behaviors associated with addiction; or they may already be homeless and seek out relief from their stressful situation by starting to use drugs.

People who are homeless may use the library more frequently and for greater lengths of time than people who have homes, schools, and places of employment. The library services that homeless populations seek out may be our most essential services, including a warm place to stay when it is cold, a cool place to stay when it is hot, restrooms, and comfortable seating. With just these simple services, libraries can provide tremendous support. Moreover, just because someone is homeless does not mean that they will have behavior issues or be disruptive to library services.

When someone who is homeless also struggles with addiction, they may be more likely to purchase their drugs at the library or near the library. They may also be more likely to use their drugs in the library, as well as find ways to obtain money in the library through such means as panhandling, theft, and prostitution. The more aware staff are of everyone in the library, the easier it is to identify and correct these problem behaviors while continuing to offer support.

Veterans and Addiction

One of the most shocking realizations I had while working with people struggling with addiction at the library was the number of veterans and their family members who were seeking assistance. Substance abuse is a growing problem for servicemen and women due to the physical and mental health problems and disabilities arising from the traumas suffered while serving in the military (National Veterans Foundation 2016). The physical and emotional traumas that our current servicemen and women experience have become a nationwide concern as the suicide rates of veterans climb to horrific numbers. Substance use by this population could be a way to self-medicate, or deal with physical or emotional traumas when returning from service, or it could result from being prescribed pain medication for an injury.

One of the most profound moments I had in working with people struggling with addiction was meeting a young veteran who became addicted to heroin after an injury he received when serving overseas. He had initially been prescribed an opioid painkiller, and when he was no longer able to obtain this drug, he began using heroin. (It is often cheaper and easier to purchase heroin than prescription pills for pain.) He told his heartbreaking story of being injured in the line of duty, being given a prescription drug for the pain, and then finding that he could no longer afford the medication. Because he still had pain, he transitioned to heroin because of the lower price and ease of obtainment. He was now losing everything he had to addiction, but he was still using heroin, knowing that with each dose he also risked his life with a possible overdose. He wanted to stop but felt like he couldn't ask for help; he was concerned that if the military found out about his drug use, he could lose his position in the service.

It can be difficult for veterans to ask for help for a variety of reasons, but there are many great support services, like the local Veterans Affairs facilities and call centers, that can be of assistance. Meeting with your local Veterans Affairs office is a great way to gain a better understanding of the needs of local veterans and how the library can play a role in their lives.

Young Adults and Addiction

The use of opioid painkillers can result in addiction at a young age. One example from a parent was when her son was playing football in high school and injured his knee during a game. The emergency-room doctor prescribed a narcotic to assist with the pain of the injury and recommended that the boy see a specialist for further treatment. Soon, this young man's life had shifted from sports and school to the need to sustain his addiction. It didn't take him long to make the switch from pain medication to heroin because of the ease of obtaining the drug. His mother felt that she had no choice but to have him removed from the house due to his constant thefts and violent outbursts toward her and her other children.

Young people can start experimenting with drugs at a surprisingly early age, and understanding the signs of addiction and cultivating relationships with these young people can be crucial in identifying a substance use disorder early on. You should never dismiss drug use as a possible cause for concern simply because of the age of a young adult or child.

When a young adult becomes addicted, this immediately becomes part of the family dynamic because that person is underage and living under someone's guardianship. Parents may notice an issue with their child and seek out assistance from others to better understand if the problems are substance-related. Alternatively, they may discover the problem when they are notified by the school or police that the child has gotten into trouble for using or possessing a controlled substance, or when the child's addiction-related behavior has necessitated intervention of some sort. The library can support these parents and young adults by letting the community know that it can be a resource. Libraries can offer resource guides and programming that are focused on young adults and addiction. Collaborating with police, schools, and local organizations (YMCAs, teen centers, etc.) to promote prevention and resources for recovery are great opportunities to assist young adults and their families.

The Elderly and Addiction

When we think about those who have a substance use disorder, often the last group to enter our minds is the elderly population. For many years, I worked with a social service agency that addressed protective services for seniors (i.e., reports of abuse and neglect) and arranged for home-based services for seniors who were mostly independent, but who required assistance with things like shopping, housecleaning, cooking, bathing, and managing medication. It was very common for me to enter someone's home and find that they had pill bottles scattered across tabletops for a variety of health conditions, prescribed by various doctors. These elderly people had little or no understanding what each drug was for, what its side effects might be, and how often the drug should be taken. Seniors are often prescribed benzodiazepines for anxiety, pain, or insomnia. The National Council on Alcoholism and Drug Dependence states that there are 2.5 million older adults with an alcohol or drug problem. The council also reports that widowers over the age of 75 have the highest rate of alcoholism in the United States (National Council on Alcoholism and Drug Dependence 2018). It can be easy to overlook addiction in older adults because the symptoms can be confused with the symptoms of normal aging or prescribed medication. Seniors are frequently active library users, and it is important to be aware that addiction is an issue for this demographic as it is for others. A senior sleeping at the library could just be taking a quick nap, or they could be having a potential overdose or some other medical issue. Talking openly about addiction to elderly populations can help seniors and their families identify addiction and seek out treatment. I met one senior at the library who had struggled with alcohol addiction throughout most of his life. He was now in his 70s and had been sober for the last five years. I would often hear him speak to others in the community area of the library about his experiences, and in so many instances those he spoke to would respond by telling him of their own struggles or their concerns for a loved one. He would share some of the resources he used and was still using and would point me out as a person to trust and talk to for more information.

Caregivers of People with a Substance Use Disorder or in Recovery

Addiction can take a massive toll on the lives of those who depend on or care for people who are struggling with addiction. No matter what the structure of the family or support system of the person with a substance use disorder is, all of its members can be deeply affected by the person's addiction. Those who have a loved one struggling with addiction need support to help them care for their loved one and for themselves. There are many agencies that provide treatment for people with addiction and their families at the same time. There are also organizations that just focus on supporting the caregivers. Caregivers are often overwhelmed by the desire to help their loved one, the stigma of the disease, and the fear of losing the person to an overdose. The library can often provide contact information to these individuals, resource guides for additional resources, and contacts for public safety officers or other key people in the community who offer support services.

Children of People with a Substance Use Disorder or in Recovery

The children of people with a substance use disorder may be either aware or unaware of their parent's struggle. Children born to mothers who were using drugs while pregnant can face a lifetime of physical, mental, and emotional difficulties.

Social service agencies can assist the family or remove the children from a household where a child may not be properly cared for. In some cases, the children will live with the parent in the rehabilitation facility. If the children live in a home where a parent is using drugs, the environment can be unstable and place the children at risk of physical, verbal, and emotional abuse. Parents struggling with addiction may neglect the needs of their children, especially those who are not old enough to care for themselves.

If library staff are concerned that a child is not being cared for or is in danger, it is important to take action and notify the proper authorities. In some states, librarians are mandated reporters for suspected child abuse or neglect.

Individuals Who Are Grieving after a Death from an Overdose

Death is a traumatic event for those who cared for an individual with a substance use disorder, and death due to an overdose can result in a complex grieving process. Those who lose someone to an overdose may feel that their loved one was not seen as important, or as deserving of grief by the community. They may feel isolated and less likely to communicate about their loss and grief because of the stigma associated with addiction. Over the years, an increasing number of obituaries have honored those who succumbed to addiction by acknowledging the disease and the fight that they lost. These obituaries are heartbreaking and powerful statements of love by their families.

It is often initially unclear if a death due to drugs was the result of a suicide or an accidental overdose. It takes time for the medical examiner to make that determination, and there are times when the cause remains undetermined. There are also instances when those who cared for the individual who died were unaware of the person's substance use until their death. Because many people who struggle with substance use addiction become socially isolated, there are also times when the victim's body is not immediately found or is found in a public or abandoned space. If there was someone around when the overdose occurred, they might have made unsuccessful efforts (CPR, naloxone, etc.) to revive the person, which can be very traumatic for them.

After losing someone to an overdose, the survivor may feel a strong desire to gain an understanding of what happened to their loved one. The person may research substance use disorders and prevention in an effort to figure out what they might have been able to do to prevent the overdose. They may also want to determine who was to blame or who can be held accountable for the overdose. They may feel anger toward the deceased, other caregivers, themselves, toward the lack of local support, or toward the phenomenon of addiction in general. Fear of losing another loved one to an overdose can also be a significant concern if they have other family members with a substance use disorder, or if they were unaware that their loved one was using drugs and now fear being unable to identify whether or not another member of the family is using drugs. The library can support grieving individuals by providing a welcoming space that will support their need for information about substance use and also assuage their grief. The library may also be able to connect them with appropriate support organizations.

Listen, Respond, Educate

Whoever you are working with in the library, it is important to listen to the issues and concerns they have and respond in a way that meets or exceeds their expectations. In addition, the library should always be working to educate the public about what the library is, the services it provides, and its expectations regarding both patron and staff behavior. Never assume that everyone knows what a library has to offer; you can be the positive and helpful introduction to libraries that everyone deserves.

REFERENCES

National Council on Alcoholism and Drug Dependence. 2018. "Alcohol, Dependence and Seniors." www.ncadd.org/about-addiction/seniors/alcohol-drug-dependence-and-seniors.

National Veterans Foundation. 2016. "What Statistics Show about Veteran Substance Abuse and Why Proper Treatment Is Important." https://nvf.org/veteran-substance-abuse-statistics/.

Psychology Today. 2018. "Co-Occurring Disorders." www.psychologytoday.com/us/conditions/co-occurring-disorders.

Substance Abuse and Mental Health Services Administration. 2018. "2017 NSDUH Annual National Report." www.samhsa.gov/data/report/2017-nsduh-annual-national-report.

4
Behavior and Stigma

ONCE YOU KNOW SOME OF THE SIGNS OF ADDICTION, YOU MAY be able to identify people with a substance use disorder who are using your library and find ways to assist them while they are there. Don't focus on trying to be 100 percent sure the person is using drugs or trying to determine what drugs they might be using. The librarian's role at this time is not to play Sherlock Holmes or Nancy Drew; it is to understand that there is a patron in distress who may need additional observation, redirection, and services. Moreover, the typecasting of a person as being a "difficult patron" does not benefit anyone. The fact that someone is struggling not to use a drug that they know could kill them at any time does not make them a difficult patron. It makes them a person in distress.

Focusing on behavior rather than appearances is critical with addiction because addiction affects the rich and the poor alike, and those with and without support systems. The person using drugs may be dirty, disheveled, and smelly, or they may dress at the height of fashion with designer clothes and beautifully styled hair. If you have a patron who is visibly anxious, euphoric, paranoid, confused, hallucinating, speaking very rapidly or very slowly, is barely conscious, or is struggling to stay awake, these are all signs that should not be ignored because they could be a sign of a serious medical need. (For a list of common behaviors for specific drug use, see appendix A.)

These signs and symptoms are opportunities for you to approach a patron and ask if they are okay and if there is anything you can do to assist them. In most instances they will say no, but the interaction gives you the opportunity to let them know you are aware of them in the building. If they say yes, an even greater opportunity may become available and you can offer them help with library resources. In other instances, the patron's behavioral problems become more evident after you've made your approach, and then you can take additional steps to address the behavior and let them know what local resources are available to them.

Admittedly, it is not easy to start these conversations. When I started forcing myself to talk to people who were behaving abnormally, I was terrified. My hands and voice would shake, I would sweat, and I would try to talk myself out of it by saying that this was not in my job description and that the person would probably be fine. Then I would take a deep breath and remind myself that providing access to services includes engagement with all people who might need services. Over time I became much more confident, comfortable, and even bold when talking to patrons about my concern for them.

I compare this situation to patrons who are viewing pornography on the library's public computers. The first time I saw someone looking at porn on a computer I wanted to run away. I was only in my early 20s, and I was horrified at the thought of having to tell a man in his 50s to not look at pornography. But I knew I had to do this for the sake of the other patrons using the library. I wanted the library to be a welcome space for everyone, and his viewing of pornography was certainly not making it a welcome space for me. That first time I confronted a patron was awful, but in each instance after that I became more confident. Confidence comes through action, and even practicing these moments with a friend or coworker can help prepare you for a real-life interaction.

Respecting the Person

When working with people with a substance use disorder, please remember to always treat them with respect and dignity. No one chooses the path of addiction for themselves and as librarians, we are there to support them. Addiction carries so much stigma, shame, and discrimination; it is our role to push past this and work with the facts. The impact of stigma is one of the reasons it is important to think about people struggling with addiction as people who are in distress. Stigma is one of the reasons so many people will not ask for the help they so desperately need.

When I was in high school in the 1990s, I had a friend who contracted AIDS and a few years later died from the disease. He was a funny, charming, and relentlessly happy person. He spoke openly about having AIDS because of his fear of passing it to another person, but he lied to his family and many of his friends about how he had contracted the virus. He had contracted the virus through a same-sex relationship. He felt strongly that his family could accept his contracting AIDS through intravenous drug use, but not if the infection had resulted from his sexual practices as a gay man. The stigma attached to him because people believed that he was using drugs stayed with him throughout the rest of his life, and many members of his support system stayed away due to what they thought were his poor life choices and lack of self-control, along with their fear of contracting the virus themselves. My friend's fear of being condemned for homosexuality led him to choose one horrible stigma and life of discrimination over another while additionally being stigmatized for being sick. I often think of him when I work with the public Stigma can arise from fear and from people not having enough information about the illness. As library workers and as human beings, we need to try to change this so that people can receive the treatment, empathy, and love they deserve.

> **LANGUAGE AND ADDICTION**
>
> One way in which we can respect people with a substance use disorder is to pay attention to the language that we use when discussing those who are struggling with addiction and recovery. When we use terms like "drug user," "drug addict," "addict," "junkie," "dopehead," or "stoner," we reinforce the notion that people struggling with addiction are morally weak, of low character, or dangerous. Instead we should identify someone as "a person with [specific issue]." We should use terms like "a person with a substance use disorder," "a person struggling with addiction," "a person in recovery," or "a person with drug (or alcohol) dependence." This change in terminology has been positive for other stigmatized groups such as people with disabilities and people with mental health disorders. Labeling someone as "mentally ill" as opposed to a "person with a mental health disorder" has a different tone and message, and this is the same as labeling someone as an "addict" as opposed to "someone with a substance use disorder."

Disruptive Behaviors

When I first witnessed disruptive behaviors in the library, I would try to determine if the behavior was part of a substance addiction or a mental health issue. I spent a great deal of time going through old notes, books, and experiences from my time working in the field of psychology and social services and then comparing this material to what I was learning about addiction, different drugs, and the behavioral signs I was observing in the library. I was trying to combine my past work in social services with my current work as a reference librarian, but I was making a mess out of trying to diagnose the patrons. I had so many patrons from both drug rehabilitation facilities and mental health facilities using the library that I even asked the workshop leader Warren Graham how I might tell the difference between addiction and mental illness. Warren jokingly replied that the solution to my concerns was to find another job. Later, when I was documenting inappropriate behaviors, it dawned on me that the causes of the behavioral issues that I was trying to understand so desperately were truly not critical to the work I was trying to do. In that library setting, it was simply impossible for me to separate behavior resulting from drug use from that arising from mental health problems. I realized that my treatment of all such patrons should be the same, and the only real difference would be in what needs they expressed while I was working with them.

People struggling with addiction or mental health problems may exhibit behavioral issues every time they use the library, or they may never do anything that would require your attention. This is why it is best to separate the person from the behavior. When there are behaviors in the library that are of concern, the first thing you must do is correct the behavior that is causing the disruption. Whether you have a patron running through the building who tells you he is being chased by a vampire, or another patron who is just pacing back and forth across the library endlessly, the behavior needs to be addressed. If you are concerned about your safety or the safety of others in the library, then you should immediately contact emergency personnel. If you feel that you can address the behavior, ask yourself if the behavior is causing a disturbance in the library. If it is, then ask the patron if they are okay. If they state that they are, ask them to refrain from the specific activity because it is disturbing other people's ability to use the library. When you ask if they are okay, they might explain that their behavior is due to a physical or mental health condition. In this case, it might be helpful to think of a way to help this patron find a place to pace—perhaps in the back of the stacks or on the sidewalk outside, instead of in the main areas of the building. By contrast, I have never had anyone tell me that their behavior was caused by an addiction, though in some cases I strongly believed it was. But no matter what the cause of the behavior, you need only to focus only on the behavior that is the concern and correct that issue.

5
Library Safety and Security

AS THE DIRECTOR OF A PUBLIC LIBRARY, I HAVE HAD TO SAY over and over again that the library is a public space—but that doesn't necessarily mean it is a safe space. Since everyone is welcome, *everyone* is welcome. Everyone includes children, young adults, adults, and the elderly. Everyone includes both the heartwarming child who is discovering new genres and the registered sex offender who is seeking employment opportunities by attending a job seekers program. Everyone includes those who check out their books and never say more than three words to anyone and those who spend their entire day in the library talking to anyone who will listen.

Earlier this year, a 22-year-old woman studying at the Winchester Library in Massachusetts died after being stabbed by a 23-year-old man. After the attack, several news sites reported that he was known by the townspeople and the local police for having mental health issues but was repeatedly treated and not thought to be a risk to anyone's safety (Arsenault and Crimaldi 2018). The man was later diagnosed with schizophrenia (Andersen 2018). In response to incidents like this, the public is becoming more aware of the sometimes random—and sometimes intentional—acts of violence that can occur in public spaces or spaces where large groups of people congregate.

Libraries are stereotyped as being filled with quiet people who are reading, researching, relaxing, and enjoying the peaceful atmosphere. Libraries are often scenes of incredibly diverse usage, and I find people enjoying the library in different ways every time I walk through the building. But I also remember that our libraries are public spaces which are reflections of our communities. And both people and communities have their own strengths and struggles.

Preventing an Overdose

One significant concern for libraries that provide services to people struggling with addiction is the possibility of an overdose or even a death in the library. At this time there are no statistics for the number of overdoses that occur in libraries, or the number of deaths due to an overdose in the library. But if you search on the topic of "overdoses in libraries," you can undoubtedly see the seriousness of the problem. Librarians are now in the trenches with people struggling with addiction and recovery, trying to create a welcoming place for them.

According to the Centers for Disease Control, more than 70,000 people died from an overdose in 2017. This is a 316 percent increase over the overdose death rate in 1999. The most common overdose drugs are opioids. (See figure 5.1.)

FIGURE 5.1 / Drugs involved in U.S. overdose deaths, 1999-2017

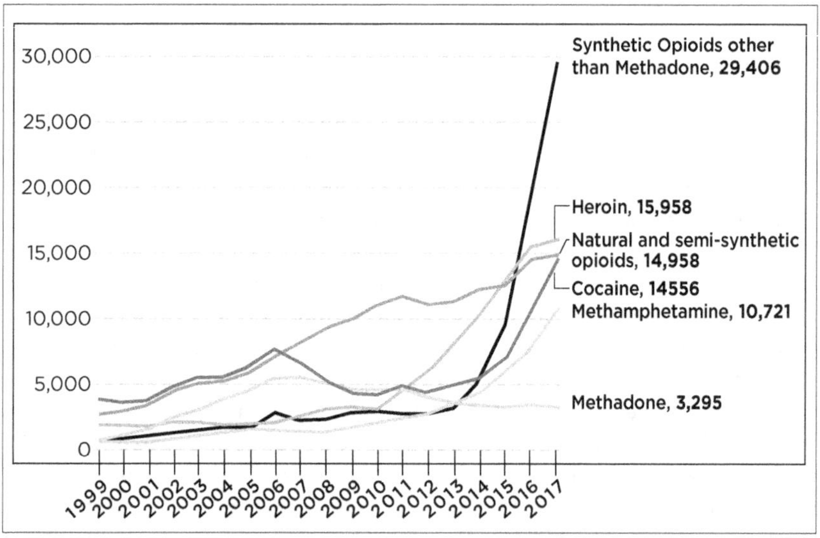
30,000
25,000
20,000
15,000
10,000
5,000
0
1999
2000
2001
2002
2003
2004
2005
2006
2007
2008
2009
2010
2011
2012
2013
2014
2015
2016
2017
Synthetic Opioids other than Methadone, 29,406
Heroin, 15,958
Natural and semi-synthetic opioids, 14,958
Cocaine, 14556
Methamphetamine, 10,721
Methadone, 3,295

SOURCE: National Institute on Drug Abuse. 2019. "Overdose Death Rates." www.drugabuse.gov/related-topics/trends-statistics/overdose-death-rates.

LIBRARY SAFETY AND SECURITY / 27

FIGURE 5.2 / Overdose deaths from fentanyl nationwide

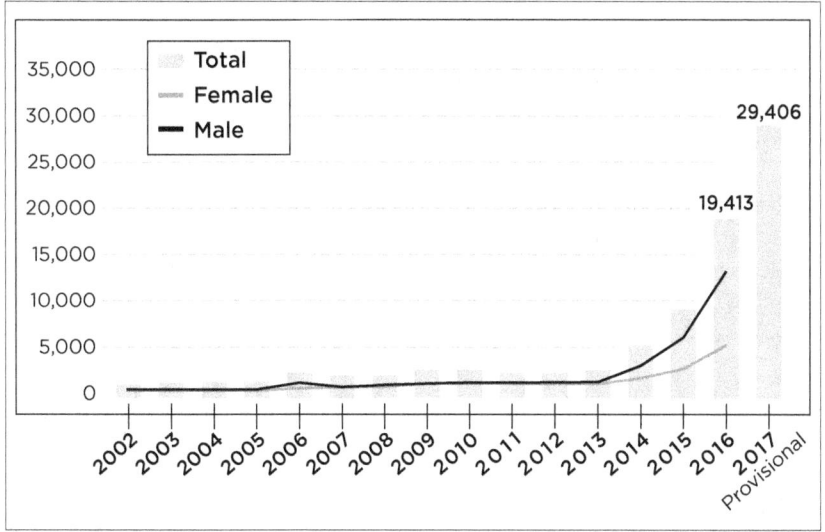

SOURCE: National Institute on Drug Abuse. 2019. "Overdose Death Rates." www.drugabuse.gov/related-topics/trends-statistics/overdose-death-rates.

The synthetic opioid fentanyl has become a national concern because even a tiny amount of the drug can result in death from an overdose. Figure 5.2 from the National Institute on Drug Abuse shows the devastating effect fentanyl is having on the number of overdose deaths nationwide.

With the increased availability and use of opioids leading to so many overdose deaths, libraries have the opportunity to step up and try to save the lives of those who are visiting their facilities.

Naloxone can be used to counter the effects of an opioid overdose. It can be administered to anyone who is unconscious, and it will only have an effect on the individual if they have used an opioid. So, if a person has used an opioid and another drug, naloxone will just reverse the effects of the opioid and the person will still be affected by the other drug. If a person has not used drugs and naloxone is administered, it will have no effect (Naloxoneinfo.org 2018). Naloxone is available in a nasal spray (Narcan) and in injection form (Evzio).

When I went to a local pharmacy to inquire about naloxone, the pharmacist suggested the injection form and showed me how to administer it. The prescription came with two injectors and a training kit to practice administering the drug.

The use of naloxone in the public library is still a controversial issue. I view naloxone in the same way that I view a defibrillator. I hope that I never have to use either one, but I also never want to be in doubt about my ability

> **LOCATING NALOXONE**
>
> NaloxoneNow is an app created by the drug manufacturer that tells you where the drug can be obtained and provides a step-by-step how-to guide for the nasal spray, a video guide on how to use the nasal spray, general safety information, and a link to call 911 (iMedicalApps.com 2018).
>
> The website DontDie.org also provides information about naloxone, including a detailed video that explains how to identify an overdose, the steps to take if someone may have overdosed, how to use both the nasal spray and injectable naloxone, educational resources, and how to find treatment (Baltimore City Health Department 2018).

to use them effectively and safely. I also know that if someone needed either one, I could live with the fact that I did everything I could for that person, and I would deeply regret it if I had the opportunity to help and did not take it. Choosing to carry naloxone is not putting out a welcome mat for people to use drugs and to overdose. It is choosing to fight for people struggling with addiction, by giving them another chance to recover.

Some libraries will carry naloxone for the staff to use, while others will not for a variety of reasons. In the library I work at now, the board of trustees voted against having the drug available for staff in the library, so I let the board know of my decision to carry the drug on my person, and that I was doing so as a private citizen and not as an employee of the library. I also told the staff that I was carrying naloxone as a citizen, and if there was an instance when someone was having a medical emergency they should (as always) notify me, and if I suspected it was due to an overdose I would use the naloxone. Several staff members expressed interest in obtaining naloxone for themselves.

> **IF THERE IS AN OVERDOSE IN YOUR LIBRARY**
>
> If you observe a patron who is unconscious or has a difficult time waking up, has slow or shallow breathing, or has blue or purple fingertips or lips, it may mean that they are overdosing. Here is what you should do:
>
> 1. Stay with the person and try to wake them up or keep them conscious.
> 2. Ask someone to call 911 for emergency services.
> 3. If you have naloxone, administer it. Rescue breathing or CPR may be administered while waiting for emergency services.

Creating Safe Spaces

Library bathrooms are a common location where people will go to purchase and use drugs because of the privacy available there. There may be some physical signs of drug use there, including discarded drug paraphernalia, nip bottles, or needles. Needles left where people might be injured have become such a significant issue for some libraries that sharps containers have been installed in the bathrooms. Bathrooms are also the site where overdoses commonly occur. If your library's bathrooms are an area of concern, consider locking the rooms and allowing access to them with a key. New technologies are coming forward to help fight the crisis. A Massachusetts company has created a device that will alarm staff if someone goes into a restroom and then stops moving for a predetermined amount of time (Capelouto 2018). Another technique being implemented at rest stops, grocery stores, and some libraries to reduce overdose rates is to switch to blue lighting in restrooms, which makes it more difficult for someone trying to find a vein to inject drugs. However, one study done by the *Harm Reduction Journal* reported that half of all people who were using a restroom to inject drugs would do so despite the blue lights (Crabtree et al. 2013). Moreover, I question the stigmatizing effect this lighting technique might have on people struggling with a substance disorder and how it may affect the general public's ability to use the restroom safely.

It cannot be stressed enough that the public library is a public space and so will never truly be a safe space. But there are many things libraries can do to increase safety: they can avoid having unstaffed areas, remain aware of the actions of visitors, and know what to do when something does happen. Being prepared could save someone's life.

REFERENCES

Andersen, T. 2018. "Winchester Library Stabbing Suspect Has Schizophrenia, Lawyer Says." *Boston Globe,* April 11. https://bostonglobe.com/metro/2018/04/11/alleged-killer-woman-inside-winchester-library-diagnosed-with-schizophrenia-lawyer-says/kbXkoWX5LSZtca25Fm7U3H/story.html.

Arsenault, M., and L. Crimaldi, 2018. "Police Records on Winchester Suspect Detail Odd, Threatening Behavior." *Boston Globe,* March 7. https://www.bostonglobe.com/metro/2018/03/07/accused-winchester-killer-had-two-dozen-run-ins-with-police-past-six-years/QUM5FErlsjf7g3YM7mrY7L/story.html.

Baltimore City Health Department. 2018. "You Can Stop Overdose Deaths." http://dontdie.org.

Capelouto, J. D. 2018. "Anti-Motion Detector Preventing Overdose-Related Deaths in Public Bathrooms." *Boston Globe,* June 26. www.bostonglobe.com/metro/2018/06/26/anti-motion-detector-aims-prevent-overdoses-public-bathrooms/xQEHDyAkcBuMQRFKhAbI4H/story.html.

Crabtree, Alexis, Gareth Mercer, Robert Horan, Shannon Grant, Tracy Tan, and Jane A. Buxton. 2013. "A Qualitative Study of the Perceived Effects of Blue Lights in Washrooms on People Who Use Injection Drugs." *Harm Reduction Journal* 10, no. 22 (October 8). www.ncbi.nlm.nih.gov/pmc/articles/PMC3853159/#__ffn_sectitle.

iMedicalApps.com. 2018. "NARCAN Now: A Free Guide to the Use of a Potential Life-Saving Treatment for Opioid Overdose." www.imedicalapps.com/2018/07/narcan-now-a-free-guide-to-the-use-of-a-potential-life-saving-treatment-for-opioid-overdose/.

Naloxoneinfo.org. 2018. "Naloxone: Frequently Asked Questions." http://naloxoneinfo.org/sites/default/files/Frequently%20Asked%20Questions-Naloxone_EN.pdf.

6

Library Policies

LIBRARIES HAVE MANY DIFFERENT POLICIES THAT REGULATE actions by both the staff and the public, including ones for collection development, circulation, internet/computer use, behavior, and child safety. The policies that regulate behavior, child safety, and social media use are important to have in any circumstances, but they can be critical to avoid or correctly handle problematic situations when working with people struggling with addiction. If well thought-out, clearly written, and reviewed and approved by the administration, these policies can strengthen the library's relationship with the public, the staff, and other departments.

Behavior Policy

A strong library policy can assist your staff in correcting patrons' behaviors and reaching out for safety assistance when necessary. Every library should have a clear and precise policy to specify appropriate behavior in the library. Libraries should not assume that everyone understands what a library is for and what services it provides. As a reflection of their communities, different libraries will vary in the behavior they expect from patrons. One library will allow cell phone use or food and drink, and another will not.

Before my library had a behavior policy, I struggled with inappropriate patron behavior. But after reading *The Black Belt Librarian: Real-World Safety & Security* (2011) by Warren Graham, I started making changes. First, I made sure that I always knew who was in the library (or at least on my floor of the library) and what they were doing. In this way, I was able to identify and correct behavior issues as they occurred. Every thirty minutes, I would get out from behind my desk and walk the floor from one end to the other. Being more observant meant that I had an increased number of incident reports, but it also meant that I was finding more people looking at pornography, eating food, sleeping, or being disruptive to others. I also saw many people browsing the library that I could offer assistance to with ease, and most times they took me up on my offer.

After noticing the problems occurring at the library, my next obstacle was understanding what I could or could not do to stop the behaviors I was encountering. The biggest problem was that we had no behavior policy. In reality, nothing was telling the patrons or the staff that any behavior was inappropriate. We had a few signs up telling people not to use their cell phones and not to eat or drink in the building, but we had no formal policy in place. We had a computer use policy which told people that viewing pornography was inappropriate, but I had nothing to back me up to stop people from doing this. I would have to tell the same person several times a day (and every day) to stop looking at pornography. It was making my work environment an unwelcoming place, and I felt frustrated by my inability to stop the behavior.

In response to this problem, my library quickly began the process of writing and implementing a behavior policy, and with that policy I felt empowered and strengthened. Now I could tell a patron to leave the building for the day, and after repeated offenses I could work with the library director to ban that patron for weeks, months, or even a year. It didn't take long for the patron who was regularly viewing pornography to receive a long-term ban from the building. I hate having to tell someone that they must leave and not come back into the building for some time, but thanks to a clear and simple policy that is made available to everyone, I know it is the patron who has gotten themselves banned, not me. It was their behavior that resulted in their limited access to the library. With each experience, I always hope that the person will return but that the problematic behavior will not.

People struggling with addiction can often be disruptive or participate in illegal behavior in the library or on the grounds. It is critical that before you try to address any of these issues, you have a patron behavior policy. Before you take any steps to work with your patrons, I strongly urge you to either create or review your library's behavior policy. Don't wait until you have a problem and then wish you had a policy in place. The public needs to have the policy to ensure that you have a welcoming library that they can use, and the staff needs to have the policy to back them up when a patron's behavior in the library is inappropriate. The behavior policy should be available for patrons to take copies of, it should be on the library's website, and it should be distributed to all patrons when they get new library cards. I have welcomed to my library many adults who have never even been to a library before. I am always surprised by how many adults do not know what services a library provides. I always explain how the lending system operates, and I stress that we have spaces and technology for them to use, as well as materials for them to borrow, events that are free to attend, and so much more. I also explain the behavior that is expected of them.

There may be specific behaviors that you want to bring to everyone's attention or that are a prominent issue for your library, and you certainly can mention those in the policy. One possibility could be sleeping in the public library. The library as a warm and welcoming place can be so relaxing that people can fall asleep. But one sign of an overdose is a loss of consciousness, so if a patron is sleeping, they might be experiencing an overdose or another medical emergency such as diabetic shock. Any patron who is not conscious is a potential safety concern. I have read about many academic libraries offering places for students to sleep, and that would have been wonderful when I was a student but now, as a library director who has seen sleeping patrons who are actually in need of medical assistance, I would be very concerned about the risk of allowing sleeping in a library, because patrons who are not aware of their surroundings while in a public space are at a higher risk of experiencing a negative incident.

The library's behavior policy should not only inform the public and staff what behaviors are not allowed at the library, but also spell out the consequences of such inappropriate behavior. Having the ability to tell someone they must leave the library for the day and knowing that my action was backed up by the behavior policy gave me the ability to maintain control in the library. If someone pushed back on this decision, I had the policy on hand to support me and educate the patron. The consequences of inappropriate behavior should be specific, so that the public knows that such behavior will lead to a loss of library privileges, and that if the behavior reoccurs even more library privileges will be withdrawn. But the policy should also be flexible enough so that the punishment fits the offense. For example, if someone is using a cell phone in an area where it is prohibited, I would first inform the person that use is not permitted and tell them where they can use their phone. If they continue to use their phone inappropriately, I would tell them that they need to leave for the day. But if a patron threw a book across the room, I would just tell them to leave immediately.

> **WHEN TO INVOLVE THE POLICE**
>
> Any inappropriate behavior that is illegal should immediately be reported to the police. I experienced two incidents that involved solicitation for sex at the library, and I did not approach the patron but immediately called the police. I tell my staff that if there is ever a moment when they think the police should be called for suspicious activity, or when they feel unsafe, they should always call the police. The police would agree that it is always better to call and have no issue than not to call and have a serious incident occur.

Child Safety Policy

Child safety is a second area that you will want to address in your behavior policy or in a separate policy. Promoting early literacy and a lifelong love of reading to children is one of the most precious and vital things that libraries do, and we should encourage this as much as possible. The library is welcome to everyone, including children and other vulnerable populations. You should talk to the schools and police and research your community to determine what restrictions you want to set regarding child safety. I recommend setting both a minimum age at which children may visit the library unattended and a minimum age for caregivers who are in charge of supervising children. Libraries don't want to tell people how to parent, but for safety reasons, they also don't want children unattended.

Media Policy

Library interactions with the media should also be covered through a policy or through specified procedures. The policy should include the press and various forms of social media. It is important to know who will be speaking for the library (usually the director), and who will speak for the library if the director is unavailable. The policy should also specify what information the staff should (or should not) post on social media sites about incidents that occur at the library. For example, while I was working at the library and the director was on vacation, we discovered the solicitation of prostitution by a patron in the library. The police were notified and the patron was arrested. Shortly afterward, news reporters arrived and were asking to talk to staff and patrons. Having a social media policy provides guidelines to the staff on how to handle situations like this. It is important that the library has just one voice when communicating important information to the community. Staff may have different viewpoints, which should be respected, but when it comes to the messages that come from the library, these should be well thought-out and intentional. When discussing a specific incident that has occurred in the library, it is important to understand what information can be communicated to outside groups or individuals. Libraries respect patron confidentiality, and just because a patron's behavior results in an incident that people become aware of does not negate that person's right to privacy. The incident may also be part of a police investigation and so should not be discussed with the public.

The library can counter the stigma that is associated with people with substance use disorders and their use of library services by informing the public about what is happening at the library and what the library is doing about it. It is up to the library to shape the message that is communicated. I have heard the term "radical transparency" used before, and I love this idea of extreme openness of communication practiced by public libraries. Being completely honest and open about what is happening can only educate the community about its members' needs. However, some members of the public might fear the library becoming a welcoming space for everyone, and they might express their concerns through the media. Responding to these messages on social media pages (like community Facebook pages) can be challenging because it often just adds fuel to the situation. It can be more effective to reach out to the person making the comments and ask them to have a one-on-one conversation or attend a trustees meeting, so that they can express their concerns and you can respond. In general, your comments made on library social media pages or in the local press should be well thought-out and should invite discussion. In some states online communication may be considered part of the public record, and so it cannot be deleted and must be backed up for retention.

Writing the Policy

The purpose of any policy is to inform the public and support the staff about the rules that are necessary for the library to service everyone. All library policies for the public should be written for learners. The language used in the document should have a minimum of technical and legal terms, and abbreviations should be avoided. The policy should be no longer than one page. The policy should be simple and understandable to everyone. It is important that for any restriction that is put in place, libraries should ask themselves why it is necessary. Is the rule for the public's benefit, for the staff's benefit, or because it is just the way the library has always done things? Moreover, policies should be educational, rather than a barrier to service. It is important to understand what rules may create a barrier to access or services and try to avoid adopting these.

The behavior policy does not need to list every "no" that you want to enforce. My favorite statement in our behavior policy is: "Any behavior that creates a disturbance, hinders library function, or compromises the safety of staff or patrons is prohibited." This one sentence covers just about every troublesome behavior that our patrons are capable of. My library's policy also has a line that states: "Engaging in any act or conduct which is prohibited by Federal and State law, or the Charter, Bylaws or Ordinances of the Town of _____ is forbidden." This line covers substance use in the building whether or not it is disturbing anyone, since it is against the law.

Reviewing and Approving Policies

No policy is ever going to be perfect, and you will need to revise your policy as your community and library change. After writing the first draft, send out the draft to all library staff. It is the staff who spend the most time on the front lines, and they will be able to tell you what their major concerns are and how the library can best support them. Any policy that deals with dictating and disciplining public behavior should be reviewed, if possible, by your local police department, because it is helpful for the police to be aware of the library's rules and the consequences if those rules are not followed. It was incredibly helpful for me to sit down and go over the library's behavior policy with my local police chief. The chief and I were able to talk about our mutual concerns and make any needed changes to the draft before I presented it to the trustees. This collaboration resulted in a stronger policy for the library and a better understanding between the library and the police department regarding public safety and areas of vulnerability.

Then the draft should be submitted to the library's board of trustees or other governing authority so that they can provide feedback on it. After incorporating this information, you should review the document again. Because this policy will determine what behaviors are inappropriate and what actions library staff will take to stop them, your local legal counsel should also review the document. Frankly, you want to be sure that your policy and actions do not violate federal or state law or the charter, bylaws, or ordinances of the community you serve. After that final review, the policy should be approved and made readily available to everyone using the library.

Policy Training

Once a policy is in place, it is time to educate and train the staff about it. For some policies, it is sufficient to send out a copy of the policy along with a "confirmation of recipient" form that the staff member returns to provide evidence that they have received the policy. For other policies, such as the behavior policy, it is great to get together and role-play difficult situations that may conceivably arise and give the staff a chance to practice responding to these situations. Role-playing is awkward and most people would rather not participate in it, but the reality is that role-playing will help build confidence in everyone when something does occur. In their role-playing, the staff can practice using verbal and physical body language that comes across as professional and confident instead of timid or overbearing.

All policies should be reviewed on an annual basis by the director, the library staff, the governing board or administration, and the legal department. Policies will need to change over time, and if there is a situation that demonstrates a need to review a policy, you should do so immediately before the situation should arise again.

7

Library Services

MANY PEOPLE WITH SUBSTANCE USE DISORDERS ARE UNFAmiliar with the general services that libraries offer. Libraries can provide limitless opportunities for people to transform their lives in whatever direction the journey takes them. The services you provide to your community will vary greatly depending on whether you serve a rural or urban community, how well your library is funded and supported, the staff you have working at the library, and the outside resources that already exist in your community. You should tailor your solutions to your library and community. What is feasible in one community may not be feasible in others. You should focus on what you can do and not on what you can't do. Whatever you do, never stop fighting for your community.

Programming

Library programming has become an increasingly popular service with the public. Library programming was once commonly seen as an added service that many Friends organizations supported, but it is now becoming a core service that is funded through general operating budgets. Programs that encourage participation by people with substance use disorders, their caregivers, or the public can be on topics of interest to that population, or they can be general programs (movies, concerts, handicrafts, etc.) that these groups can be encouraged to attend. Walking up to someone who is spending a day at the library and letting them know that a movie or other program is about to start at the library, that it is free, and that they are welcome to attend can be a great way to reinforce the library's mission, which is to provide services for everyone. Here's a quick look at a few programs you might consider.

Drug Awareness Programs

In Tewksbury I wanted to offer a monthly drug awareness program. The Tewksbury Police Department and the library both received grants to support the funding of this programming. Each month, we invited a specialist from a different organization to discuss a specific topic related to substance abuse. The flyers for the monthly programs all had a similar design and branding to make it easier for the public to identify them.

Some of the topics covered at the monthly programs included:

- Trauma and addiction
- Veterans and addiction
- Drug trends
- Young adults and addiction
- Heroin addiction
- Medication misuse
- Mental health disorders and addiction

At every program, we asked attendees to fill out a survey that asked about the quality of the program, if it was their first time attending a drug awareness program at the library, how they heard about the program, when (days and times of days) they would prefer to attend future programs, what future topics they would like us to address, how often they used library services, and what their connection with the subject of addiction was. We found that when people filled out the survey, they ranked the quality of the programs as high, offered suggestions for future topics, and had diverse relationships with addiction and recovery. There were also some people who attended multiple events. I was able to introduce myself to many of the attendees as the reference librarian, and then I let them know what additional services I could provide. As a result, several people came back to me for additional information at later dates.

Bystander Training

Bystander training is a great way to educate the community and the staff, and possibly save a life. Bystander training often combines general first aid training with Narcan administration training. Boards of health and local health care organizations can often offer the training at the library for little or no cost to the library, making it a great project for collaboration.

Yoga Programs

Yoga has been shown to have many potential benefits and is increasingly being used to assist people in recovery. Yoga has been shown to "prevent relapse, reduce withdrawal symptoms and drug cravings, and provide a healthy outlet to cope with potential triggers and daily life stressors" (American Addiction Centers 2018).

Art Programs

Art programs are helpful for many people and could be offered to support patrons who have substance use disorders or are in recovery. Popular forms of art used in therapy include painting, sculpting, dancing, drawing, acting, music, and poetry (Foundations Recovery Network 2018). There are specific forms of art therapy that the library could offer with professional guidance for people with substance use disorders or for individuals in recovery. There are also several adult coloring books that focus on substance abuse recovery. Art can also be used to educate the community about addiction. Libraries can host exhibits that represent the struggle with or recovery from substance use disorders, and they can exhibit artworks created by people who have personally experienced addiction.

Book Groups

Book groups held at rehabilitation centers or at the library can focus on addiction and recovery and can help those in recovery discover (or rediscover) recreational reading, thereby introducing literacy as a way of support. Regular book groups may also choose to read fiction or nonfiction works about addiction and recovery in order to promote discussion about the issue in a nonpersonal format.

Life Skills Programming

Life skills–based programming has become popular thanks to the curiosity of the younger generation, but these programs can also be great for people in recovery. Learning life skills can help people build the skills they need to remain in recovery and care for themselves in ways they might never have been able to do in the past. Life skills can include things like cooking, sewing,

> **A LIBRARY'S RESPONSE**
>
> In Ipswich, Massachusetts, the need to create programs on the subject of substance use and prevention came to light during a strategic planning process when the library was informed about the substance use crisis in its community. The library started by talking to community partners about what was already being done and where the library might be able to fill a need. It quickly because clear to all parties that combining their resources would amplify each other's reach. The Ipswich Public Library partnered with the police, YMCA, local schools, and Ipswich Aware (a group that represents many other local organizations) and used a State Aid award, library trust funds, and the Friends of the Library to financially support a series of programs. The library created a community read program around the book *Beautiful Boy: A Father's Journey through His Son's Addiction* by David Sheff, and the author spoke at the final event. Other programs were held throughout the fall leading up to the final event and included book discussions, film screenings, panel discussions, yoga for recovery sessions, and informative lectures (Ipswich Public Library 2019). This collaborative process created relationships with organizations that will continue for future initiatives. Some of the programs that were created for this series will now be able to run again or be loaned out to other organizations.

housecleaning, basic repairs for household items, job searching, gardening, and so on.

There are endless opportunities to assist communities through programming to let your community know that you care, and to offer information that can be an integral part of prevention and recovery.

LIBRARY MATERIALS

Providing access to information and recreation through library materials is one of the core services that libraries provide. Whether this involves circulating materials at the library or setting up small collections of materials at rehabilitation and detox centers, it is crucial to make this core service available to as many people as possible.

Most of the people who enter the library looking for information and materials about addiction are those living and working with someone who has a substance use disorder. In prior years, materials about addiction were limited in quality and quantity, but now we are seeing some profound and helpful resources becoming available. These titles often go missing from the collection, and although I am always disappointed by the fact that someone felt uncomfortable checking these materials out from the library, I still hope that the materials will help those who took them. Here are a few types of materials that I've found to be of interest to those with substance abuse disorders.

Memoirs

Memoirs written by others who struggled with addiction and were able to recover are popular with people who are themselves facing the same struggle. There are many profound stories of struggle and survival that people in recovery may find inspiring. These memoirs let people know that they are not alone and that others before them have trodden the same path, and done so successfully. For those in recovery or their caregivers, knowing other people's stories can be comforting and inspirational.

Short Stories

One genre that I was surprised to find popular with people in recovery was short stories. In particular, I found that my small number of Chicken Soup for the Soul books had very high circulation and would often become worn out with use and need to be replaced. (These books are collections of short, inspirational, true stories about the lives of ordinary people.) I would purchase copies of these books for the collection and sort through donations for copies that I could add to the collection. One day, while talking with a woman in recovery who was asking about additional Chicken Soup titles, I asked her what she found so appealing about the series. She told me that recovery was horrible and that she always felt sick and was constantly trying not to use again. The stories in the series were short so that she could read one in a few sittings, and they were easy to understand and positive, which provided her with hope and inspiration. For her, these books really were "chicken soup for the soul." After speaking with this patron, I began to suggest short stories as a reading option for other patrons who were in rehabilitation programs. It was wonderful to tell people about this genre, which made reading more accessible during their recovery.

Movies and Music

Other very popular collections were movies and music. Patrons found these items to be comforting during their stay in some of the recovery programs. Because of the high popularity and the frequent late returns of these items, the library had to set stricter circulation policies on them with both institutional and temporary cards.

> **CIRCULATING MATERIALS TO THE RESIDENTS OF REHABILITATION CENTERS**
>
> Because people reside at rehabilitation centers only for a short period, the library materials they borrow are often not returned. Returning library items is simply not a priority for many of the people borrowing these items while they are in the early stages of recovery. To avoid the loss of materials and to better serve people living in these facilities, we changed our circulation policies so that a library card was issued to the rehabilitation facility, so a staff member there could be reached when materials were not returned. We also recognized that certain books would be borrowed but either not returned or stolen, and so we adjusted our collection development plans to accommodate the replacement of those materials. In addition, we purchased more materials in e-book, downloadable audio, and movie formats. These collections began to circulate quickly; they provided additional patron confidentiality, and they eliminated our concern over their theft. Another possible option would be for a library to create a small collection for the rehabilitation facility that contains donated or discarded materials that would not need to be returned to the library.

Readers' Advisory, Resource Guides, and Information Services

Readers' (and viewers' and listeners') advisory is a large part of a library's service to people with substance use disorders and their families. Talking about and recommending books is a great way to create a bond with community members, and the resulting discussions can encourage patrons to ask for additional resources and assistance. Sharing resources for recovery also demonstrates that the library is concerned about the crisis.

Resource Guides

Many of the caregivers I've spoken to at the library are looking for resources they can use to assist a family member or friend who is struggling with addiction. I decided to create a resource guide for these caregivers. This bookmark-sized guide includes a list of physical materials, online resources, and local organizations that could assist caregivers. I placed the resource guide by the reference desk as well as at the end of the shelving area in the nonfiction stacks, along with a display of some of the materials mentioned in the guide. I also listed caregiver resources so that people could find support themselves or find organizations and resources to help them while they were working to assist their loved ones. I had several patrons approach me with questions after picking up the guide.

Book Displays

During a community-wide drug awareness week, I put up a large special display of books, movies, pamphlets, and the resource guide I had created for caregivers. The display was located across from the reference desk where I worked, and I noticed many people taking glances or quickly grabbing materials from it and then leaving. I also had many people comment on the display, discussing their own recovery from drugs or alcohol or the usage and recovery of someone they knew.

I kept this display up permanently after discovering how often I would need to replenish the materials on display. The display also served as a great icebreaker. Having that display available demonstrated to the public that I understood the problem of substance abuse and was willing to talk about it.

Recommended Reading Guides

After obtaining a better understanding of the reading preferences of people in recovery, I created new resource guides listing recovery memoirs and short stories. I placed these guides in a central location and also near the location of the items in the collection. I also put all of the resource guides I had created on the library's website in digital form. In this way, I hoped to find ways to reach our virtual patrons and those who might not feel comfortable picking up a paper guide in a public location. The resource guides had recommended resources for adults who were in any stage of recovery and resources for those who have loved ones struggling with addiction or are in recovery. The resource guides recommended physical books, e-books, and films, and gave both contact information for local resources and information on how to reach out to a librarian for additional research.

Readers' advisory service was another great way for me to introduce patrons to additional information and resources. When speaking to a patron looking for addiction memoirs or to someone I suspected (through behavior and conversation) was in recovery or was caring for someone in recovery, I would offer to provide additional information on the topics of recovery and substance use.

Another great opportunity to provide information to patrons is when you need to approach someone that you suspect is using drugs, or when you need to address behaviors that are inappropriate in the library. When a patron was sleeping or acting out in the library, I would explain why the behavior was not appropriate, ask if they were okay, and, if I felt it appropriate, would offer to help them seek support or information. Speaking so directly took a bit of courage on my part in the beginning, but confidence comes through action, and over time I became much more comfortable with doing this. I found that offering more information was very important when I had an incident with a patron and had to ask them to leave the library. When I had to remove access to library services (even for a day), it felt much better to see the patron leave with the possibility of outside support rather than just leaving with a reprimand.

As a reference librarian, I was pleasantly surprised by the number of people who would accept my offer for additional information. I edited the readers' advisory guides that I had created and added information to them about local support agencies, how to get help, and online resources related to addiction. I would offer the guide to patrons when they appeared uncomfortable with a verbal discussion of substance use. The resource guide gives you a way to direct patrons to additional information while also maintaining patrons' confidentiality (and thus their comfort level).

> **PROTECTING CONFIDENTIALITY**
>
> Confidentiality is a concern for many who seek information and resources on the subject of drug use and addiction. Whether the patron is the one using drugs or is someone who cares about a loved one who is using drugs, the subject of addiction carries a stigma, and many people are too ashamed or embarrassed to broach the subject. It is important for libraries to communicate the promise of confidentiality and intellectual freedom that we provide to the public. Still, there may be barriers perceived by patrons who are seeking information, and it is important to understand and address these perceptions if possible. In small public libraries, the staff may be residents of the community, and so patrons may feel uncomfortable asking someone who they know from the community for resources. When I hired a children's librarian who was not from the community and lived outside of town, patrons who were looking for sensitive information—for example, information about cancer after a recent diagnosis, or where to find the Fifty Shades of Grey series of erotic novels—would approach her instead of the main desk staff, who were all living in the community. Printed guides to find "hot topics" or information on perceived controversial topics placed in areas away from the sight of the main desk proved to be a popular resource. These guides also included information about electronic content for these subjects. Other libraries have self-checkout stations as well as public areas for patron holds that give patrons the option to use an alias.

Social Services

With the ongoing financial cuts to social service programs, libraries have seen an increased number of patrons in crisis visiting the library, seeking assistance and looking for resources to help. Because everyone is free to spend as much time there as they need, the library is a welcome space for people who are struggling with substance use disorders, mental health disorders, and homelessness, as well as people who are dealing with health, financial, emotional, or other personal crises. Librarians, who are always working with their communities to provide access to outside resources, have seen a decline in the number of these resources and have faced an increase in demand to provide these types of services themselves. Libraries are known for providing free, confidential, and nonjudgmental services to all people without discrimination, so in many ways it seems natural for the people we serve in our communities to approach us for assistance.

According to the Illinois Chapter of the National Association of Social Workers, thirty public libraries nationwide have added social workers to their library staff (Janis 2018). Adding social workers to library staff has been a popular subject that I have discussed with other librarians when we talk about the future of library services and budgeting for future positions at the library. Social workers can work in conjunction with library security staff so that when a patron's behavior requires assistance from security, a social worker can also assist by evaluating the situation and providing support to that patron. In such cases, even when a patron's behavior results in their prohibition from the library at that moment, they are not banned from the library without receiving information about resources that may assist them. I suspect that the number of social workers providing resources in public libraries will increase with the demands placed on libraries to meet needs that will otherwise go unmet. There are also libraries that complement social workers with "peer navigators." Peer navigators are usually trained individuals who have personal experience with the areas of concern (addiction, positive HIV status, sexuality, homelessness, etc.) and so can offer honest and genuine support and understanding.

If hiring a social worker is not an option at your library, you should consider partnering with a social service agency to offer collaborative services. In my library we didn't have the funding to support hiring a social worker to provide this highly sought-after service, but when I heard that our community's reputable social service agency had lost funding to keep its location, I offered a meeting room that they could use at the library one day a week to support members of the community.

Funding Library Services

During my time working at the Tewksbury Public Library, the library dealt with significant financial cuts and was forced to apply for waivers with the state in order to retain its certification. The underfunded budget meant that extra money for materials, programs, and anything else I wanted to introduce to the library had to be funded with non-operational funding.

I started to research library funding from other sources. I began by reading articles, webinars, and books on library funding and grants. There are countless resources available that can help educate you on how to apply for grants. Now, as the director of as public library, I encourage you to always look for new opportunities to either refresh your existing knowledge or pick up further information that will be helpful. Funding is one area where you can never stop learning, and when I look back at my original requests (both denied and accepted) for funding, I am even more thankful to those who funded them, and gave the library the opportunity to do things that we would never have been able to do without their help.

Once you know what you want to fund, why you want to fund it, and how much funding is needed, reach out to local groups. In some instances these local groups may provide you with funding, while in other instances this may open the door to collaborating with them for new opportunities and new sources of funding. Collaboration with local groups might open up funding opportunities on its own because they might already have the funding available, but in exchange they may need a location to meet or additional library support.

The first local groups you reach out to should be within your municipality; this could be the school administration or the city or town government. I found a great ally in the Tewksbury Police Department and Officer Welch, who already had knowledge of some local funding sources and had grant-writing experience of her own. We each worked on grants and were each able to secure funding for substance use issues. If you are working with a municipality, other resources could be the schools, the veterans' affairs office, and the board of health.

When reaching out to outside organizations, you should research what organizations might already be working with people who have substance use disorders or are in recovery. You should consider local hospitals, acute care centers, crisis centers, and donation centers. Get creative and do some research looking at who in your community might have an interest in supporting your library's fight against addiction. Taking a drive around parts of town that you are less familiar with can yield possible allies and sources of information. The worst thing that can happen is that they will say no. If they do, I would gently ask them why and then plan on asking them again at a later date.

The services your library can provide may be extensive and involve large numbers of staff and a formal committee, or they may represent the efforts of just one librarian. Unlike many of our other services, services for people with a substance abuse disorder cannot be measured by the number of circulations or the number of people attending events. Instead, you should always keep in mind that your efforts will have an impact. The one resource guide that was taken, or the one book that was borrowed, might save someone's life.

REFERENCES

American Addiction Centers. 2018. "Using Yoga in Recovery." October 18. https://americanaddictioncenters.org/therapy-treatment/yoga.

Foundations Recovery Network. 2018. "How Art Therapy Is Used in Addiction Treatment." www.foundationsrecoverynetwork.com/art-therapy-used-addiction-treatment/.

Ipswich Public Library. 2019. "Ipswich Reads One Book 2019." https://www.ipswichlibrary.org/schedule-of-events-announced/.

Janis, Justine. 2018. "Public Library Social Work: An Emerging Field." Illinois Chapter of the National Association of Social Workers, June 11. http://naswil.org/news/chapter-news/featured/public-library-social-work-an-emerging-field/.

8

Library Outreach and Marketing

COLLABORATION IS CRITICAL WHEN YOU ARE WORKING WITH people with substance use disorders and their support systems. When I started my job as director, I spent a great deal of my first year meeting members of the community, especially key figures of the town, and reading over the notes and files of the previous director. I also made sure to attend meetings for library directors in the area. In that first year, not only did I get a better understanding of the community's thoughts and needs, but I also got invaluable assistance from the other library directors about how to navigate the significant issues of the first year. Thanks to the time I spent getting to know the community and the people involved in the community, I now have some wonderful people who I can reach out to for collaborative projects.

It is critical, whenever you do collaborate on a project, that you outline your goals, your timelines, and the resources that you will be able to devote to the project. Be realistic about what is feasible for you and your library. There can also be times when your library or another organization might initially be able to commit to a project but because of reasons outside of their control (such as staff changes, budget cuts, or emergencies), might have to cut back on participation. It is important that each organization communicate its challenges and work to overcome them or else adjust the goals of the project.

Ideas for Collaboration

Offer Your Space

Many libraries have rooms or other spaces that are used for meetings and events. If your library lacks the resources to offer programs of its own, you could reach out to other local organizations—such as the board of health, local hospital, or public safety department—to offer your meeting room as a place to host an event on the topic of substance use and addiction. Hosting an event may take little or no staff time and utilizes the space you already have available.

Host Speaking Events at the Library

If you have more staff available, the library could reach out to professionals who work in the area of substance use and invite them to speak at the library. As you become more active with organizations, groups, and people in your community on the topic of addiction, you will get to know who might be good speakers to invite into your library. It is also helpful, when collaborating with organizations, to ask if they do community outreach and who on their staff might be available for this.

Following your local news sources can also be a great resource. If an article about addiction or the opioid epidemic is written in the local press, those mentioned in the article or the journalists themselves might be good speakers to invite to the library. Many people invested in the field are willing to speak for free or for a small stipend.

Visit Local Organizations

You can visit local organizations (residential facilities or support organizations) in your community that offer assistance to people with a substance use disorder or those impacted by addiction. Tell these organizations that the library is a welcoming space for all and share specifically what the library is doing (or hopes to do) to fight addiction and support those in recovery. Tell them what services the library offers and how they can gain access to those services.

You should always try to let others know about the impact of addiction on your library, what resources and services it currently offers, and what it hopes to offer in the future (perhaps with additional funding that this organization might be able to provide). You can visit with the local leadership at schools, PTA meetings, Rotary meetings, chamber of commerce events, and other city or town committees and boards during their meeting times.

Share Your Resource Guides

The resource guides you create are not only a great tool to have on display and on hand in the library, but also throughout your community. You can share your resource guides with the groups you visit, including the public safety personnel, other town departments, local hospitals, and social service agencies. Ask local businesses if you can place some of the guides at their establishments, if not for the long term, then perhaps in the days leading up to a library program or during National Recovery Month (September). Businesses to consider include hotels, laundromats, senior housing common areas, low-income housing areas, food pantries, grocery stores, and post offices.

When the library provides outreach during local fairs, festivals, and farmers' markets, bring your resource guides and a few materials (if you can circulate items outside of the library) as part of the library's table. This can be just a part of the library's overall display of services offered, or it can be specifically dedicated to what the library is doing to fight addiction. Even just having some of the library's resource guides on hand can be helpful in opening up a dialogue with someone who is in need of support. A public health fair or open house at a residential facility or hospital would be another great place to showcase the library's efforts.

> **OVERDOSE CANDLELIGHT VIGILS**
>
> Some communities may hold Overdose Candlelight Vigils as a way to honor loved ones who have died from an overdose or experienced an overdose, or simply to support the community. These vigils may include a moment of silence, speakers, a procession, reading of names, candle-lighting, and access to information, services, and support. Overdose Vigils are a powerful place for the library to have a presence. You may be able to have a table with resources and items to circulate, or you may have the chance to speak and participate in the event. Just showing up is a bold affirmation to those in attendance that the library cares and wants to support everyone. The town of White River Junction in Vermont posted a video on YouTube about their first Overdose Vigil (on Overdose Awareness Day) on August 31, 2016, which shows how the event was organized, who participated in it, and some of the resources and services that were offered during the event (Critters Crusade 2016).

Ideas for Outreach

Many organizations are already doing some form of outreach or are providing services to people with substance use disorders and their families. Reaching out to these organizations can open up many opportunities not only for the people you are trying to serve, but also for the library and the organizations. It is common to discover that multiple organizations are trying to meet the same need—then they can collaborate and reach goals together that would have been difficult if not impossible to attain alone. These organizations are also often connected to or know of other groups and people that can help you serve people with substance use disorders.

When I met with the public safety officer in our town's police department, she provided me with a list of some organizations and their staffers that I could reach out to for additional information, support, and opportunities. I was not from the area, and even if I had been, I would most likely never have known what was available. The public safety officer knew many of the people in need and the people who could offer support in the community, and was kind enough not only to share the contact information for these resources, but to sit in on discussions to further our collaboration and maximize our efforts.

The first organization I reached out to was Learn to Cope. This is a nonprofit organization that supports the family and friends of people with substance use disorders through meetings, private forums, support groups, and other resources (Learn to Cope 2018). Through Learn to Cope, I learned a great deal about the impact of addiction on the family and friends of people with substance use disorders, and I also learned about the services the organization offers and the partners with whom it collaborates.

> **POWER IN NUMBERS**
>
> You can create a committee that includes people from local agencies and groups that work with people with a substance use disorder and their caregivers, or that work generally on public health issues. By organizing these people and having a way to communicate through meetings, conference calls, or e-mails, you can keep one another aware of local trends and concerns as well as combine your efforts to deliver services. This committee could be an informal group of colleagues that provide each other with support, or a more organized group with goals, objectives, and activities. Organizing or being part of a larger committee may increase the opportunities for resource-sharing, fund-raising, and meeting community needs more efficiently.

Outreach to Rehabilitation Facilities

The easiest and often the most effective way to market library services is by word of mouth. When I started to talk to patrons who were living in a rehabilitation facility about being welcome at the library and the ways the library could help them and their families, they would often tell the others in the facility about the library.

If you are not meeting people from these facilities, then you should research what detox, rehabilitation, and other facilities are in your area. Call each of the facilities and introduce yourself and ask for a time to meet face-to-face to discuss the services the library can provide. Hospitals often have rehabilitation facilities and can be a great way to provide services to a population with diverse needs. In some cases the facilities may not even be in your town and may be closer or more easily accessible from another public library. In that case, I would suggest collaborating with that community's library to provide services.

Since the people staying at detox and rehabilitation facilities do not typically stay there for an extended period, it will be most effective if a staff member visits the facility on a regular schedule to speak to the residents about library services. In detox facilities, the people are dealing with the physical impact of not using drugs, and they may benefit from books and movies that the library has discarded from the collection or that have been donated by the public. These materials can provide recreation for the residents of the facility. Let the people there tell you what they need and then try to find ways to fill those needs.

Outreach to Young Adults

Prevention is one area where schools, police departments, and boards of health work well together and where the library could supplement these organizations' efforts by providing services, materials, and space to assist with their efforts. Schools have taken on a much more significant role in educating teens and young adults about addiction, with school safety officers and programs that discuss substance use and the effects it can have on a person's life.

Recovery high schools—high schools explicitly designed for students who are recovering from a substance use disorder or a coexisting disorder—are starting to appear across the country. The students have the support they need to complete school and receive a diploma. The schools also offer support to the families of students (Association of Recovery Schools 2018). There are several recovery high schools in Massachusetts, and I have met with and assisted several recovery school students and staff members over the years. These schools are all dedicated to both education and long-term recovery. If there is a recovery high school near your library, I encourage you to reach out to it and offer your library's support and its collaboration ideas.

Outreach to the Media

Libraries don't need to wait until an incident occurs to begin talking about the opioid crisis and other substance use concerns. Publicizing the library's position, resources, and services can be done through newsletters, local newspapers, local television, community surveys, and pop-up libraries.

Social media provide another way to reach out to the community. In our town, the police department and the library jointly created a Facebook page for "Drug Awareness in Tewksbury" where we shared news, resources, information, events, local obituaries, and ways to reach out for help (https://facebook.com/tewksburydrugawareness/). The page was an excellent way for the police and library to share information with the public and introduce them to the library's welcoming presence and openness for discussion.

Talking about addiction may not be as fun as talking about the latest STEM programs or the next popular fiction title, but it is something we need to do with our communities. The library needs to let the community know that it is aware of the crisis and is a judgment-free zone, a place that welcomes and supports everyone no matter where they are in the substance use and recovery process. We need to let people know that we are fighting for their lives and for the lives of those they care about.

REFERENCES

Association of Recovery Schools. 2018. "What Is a Recovery High School." https://recoveryschools.org/what-is-a-recovery-high-school/.

Critters Crusade. 2016. "Overdose Awareness Candlelight Vigil." August 31. https://youtu.be/GEMFp3jn8k8.

Learn to Cope. 2018. "About Us—Our Story." www.learn2cope.org/about/.

9

Staff Training

AS YOU BEGIN TO COLLABORATE WITH LOCAL OFFICIALS AND external organizations, you should consider inviting some of these groups to the library to offer training or attend a staff meeting. It is helpful not only for the library's administration and department heads to meet and get to know these people, but for all of the library's staff members who interact with patrons. Having a chance to know local officials, the people in local organizations, and the missions and functions of these organizations will help your staff better serve the community. The more we can educate ourselves and our staff on the resources available to our patrons, the better we can serve our community. Well-informed staff will be more comfortable and confident in working with patrons who are struggling with or concerned about addiction, which is a sensitive and life-altering subject.

When I became the director of a public library, I was able to bring author Warren Graham out to the library to provide the same training to my staff that I myself had found so helpful. I also wanted other municipal departments to get a better understanding of our library's current issues and what some possible solutions might be, so I invited my library's board of trustees, the police department, and the town administration. Graham's training was a success not only because of the information he shared with us, but also because it improved the understanding between the library and other departments. There are many varieties of training available to you and your staff.

Mental Health First Aid Training

Most people are familiar with first aid courses, and many libraries offer these programs. In 2001 Betty Kitchener, a nurse specializing in health education, and Tony Jorm, a respected mental health literacy professor, created Mental Health First Aid. This training course has since been adapted for use in twenty-five countries. In the United States, the eight-hour-long course is designed to help people assist someone who is experiencing a mental health or a substance use–related crisis. The course also teaches people how to identify the risk factors and warning signs for mental health and addiction problems, strategies for how to help someone in both crisis and non-crisis situations, and where to turn for help. The classes have been tailored for adults, Spanish-speaking adults, youth, and Spanish-speaking youth (National Council for Behavioral Health 2018). Libraries can also reach out for support and education on how to better serve people with a mental health disorder from local social service agencies, hospitals, and government agencies.

Sharp and Hazardous Materials

Sharp and hazardous materials training is something that all who may handle these materials should be trained on. It is important for everyone's safety that these items are properly handled and disposed of. The Food and Drug Administration recommends a two-step process that includes placing all needles and sharps into a sharps disposal unit and then disposing of the container using community guidelines (Food and Drug Administration 2018). Other hazardous materials should be handled appropriately and cleaned with appropriate chemicals and tools. Many libraries have kits prepared for when staff need to clean up hazardous materials, such as bodily fluids.

> **PRESCRIPTION DRUG DROP BOXES**
>
> Most police departments have drug drop-off bins located just inside the police station; these can be used for medications that have been left in the library, and for any medications at home that people want to dispose of safely. There are also drug deactivation bags like Deterra that allow you to add the drug and warm water to an activated carbon that will dissolve the drug or draw it out of patches. These bags can then be thrown away in the household trash.

Overdose Prevention Training

The Substance Abuse and Mental Health Services Administration has a wonderful Opioid Overdose Prevention Toolkit (https://store.samhsa.gov/product/SMA18-4742) that I recommend you review and have available at your library. Training on responding to an overdose is also becoming part of regular first aid training; people are now trained on naloxone use in addition to general first aid, CPR, and defibrillator use. The Network for Public Health Law provides up-to-date information on naloxone access and Good Samaritan laws, including general information and current laws, and the most recent charge and immunity specifications for each state (Network for Public Health Law 2017). Some states also have laws that specifically address the need for library staff to have and administer naloxone (Maloney 2017). It would also be wise to check with any local council or law library that you have access to in order to better understand any of the legal risks associated with administering that drug.

If your library can have naloxone on-site, then training on how to use it can be incorporated into regular first aid and CPR training. Talk to your public health department or administration about how and where to obtain the drug for your library. It is important to get approval from your stakeholders before offering any training or supply of naloxone to your staff. If the library staff are in a union, then the issue of naloxone in the library may need to be addressed in any union contracts. If you are not allowed to have naloxone in the library, some staff may want to have it and use it as private citizens rather than as staff members. When you obtain the drug at the pharmacy, many pharmacists will train you on how to use it.

If there is an overdose that results in death at the library, your human resources department should offer services to the staff so they can understand and process the trauma of the event and grieve after losing a patron. The Centers for Disease Control and Prevention has information and a handout on "Helping Patients Cope with a Traumatic Event" that discusses common emotional responses to a traumatic event, how to help, and additional resources for support (Centers for Disease Control and Prevention 2018).

Off-Site and Online Training

Off-site training is another option for training your staff on how to handle overdoses and other drug-related topics. Staff can attend training at another library, a local college, hospital, rehabilitation center, or social service agency. Ask if your staff could have a tour of the building when they visit for training. While touring the facility, look at the building layout, the availability of staff, and the displays and resource guides. Talk to someone at the facility about their experiences and what they have learned, and possibly exchange contact information for additional questions or collaboration. If only one staff member can go for a visit or attend training, then have that person provide a summary of their visit to the rest of the staff at the next staff meeting, or write something up and send it to everyone in an e-mail.

Staff can also watch documentary videos or shorter videos online, and visit the websites and read the pamphlets of local organizations. The American Library Association, the U.S. National Library of Medicine, and other organizations have wonderful panel discussions and webinars on the topic of addiction as it relates to libraries. Some of these online discussions have a fee or charge associated with them, but many others are free. These sessions are wonderful to participate in or watch later when time allows, and at the person's own pace.

Creating Your Library's Own Training Program

As the opioid crisis spreads, its severity worsens, and the number of people affected continues to grow, I encourage you to build a collection of materials about addiction and make them available to all staff who work with people who have a substance use disorder. I pull together books and articles on the topic and place them where the library staff can access them at their leisure. You should also make sure that when resource guides on addiction are created for patrons, the staff familiarize themselves with these resources by reading the materials (or at least summaries and reviews of them).

I also suggest that you pull all of this information together to create a training guide. The culmination could be a resource guide similar to those made available for the public, or a training outline that requires the staff to view or read various materials. This is a great way to keep all of this information in one place and to educate new staff members.

As you develop this training, you should keep your library's stakeholders updated and informed. When appropriate, ask them for feedback and include them in the decision-making process. You should invite feedback not only from staff and trustees but also from appropriate administrative officials and legal counsel. It is important to have a variety of people provide their professional insights. As the process moves along, it is also wise to provide updates on what has been successful and unsuccessful with regard to the library's work on addiction. It is always a good idea to take any and every opportunity you can to share the successful moments that the library experiences, because all too often, all our administration hears about are the times when things do not work out. Communication is essential to keep everyone up-to-date on how the library is doing.

Keeping Current

It is critical for the library to keep current on what is happening in the areas of addiction and recovery. I have found that the easiest way to do this is by simply staying in the trenches. Keep observing and listening to the people who visit your library, keep working with the groups that you collaborate with, and keep addressing concerns when they arise. Other ways of keeping up-to-date include joining addiction/recovery organizations and groups on social media, following addiction and recovery topics in the news online, and reading professional journals and materials. WebJunction is collecting resources like news articles, professional articles, webinars, and websites from public libraries to support libraries in their efforts to serve people with substance use disorders (WebJunction 2018). The National Institute on Drug Abuse reports on emerging trends and new drugs online, and people can subscribe to receive e-mails when a new report is posted on its website (National Institute on Drug Abuse 2018).

Above all, be sure that you are always listening to the needs of your community, and never give up on your patrons in distress, even when they have given up on themselves. Fighting against addiction is everyone's fight. Libraries have proven time and time again how resilient they are, and this is an opportunity to demonstrate how our resilience can transcend this crisis. I encourage you all to take everything you know, everything you feel, everything that matters to you, embrace it with your heart, mind, and body, and then fight for it.

REFERENCES

Centers for Disease Control and Prevention. 2018. "Taking Care of Your Emotional Health." May 8. https://emergency.cdc.gov/coping/selfcare.asp.

Food and Drug Administration. 2018. "Best Way to Get Rid of Used Needles and Other Sharps." www.fda.gov/medicaldevices/productsandmedicalprocedures/homehealthandconsumer/consumerproducts/sharps/ucm263240.htm.

Maloney, Sean. 2017. "Maloney Introduced Lifesaving Librarians Act to Stop Heroin and Opioid Overdose Deaths." October 31. https://seanmaloney.house.gov/media-center/press-releases/maloney-introduces-life-saving-librarians-act-to-stop-heroin-and-opioid.

National Council for Behavioral Health. 2018. "Frequently Asked Questions." www.mentalhealthfirstaid.org/faq/.

National Institute on Drug Abuse. 2018. "Emerging Trends and Alerts." www.drugabuse.gov/drugs-abuse/emerging-trends-alerts.

Network for Public Health Law. 2017. "Resource: Legal Interventions to Reduce Overdose Mortality." www.networkforphl.org/resources_collection/2017/06/08/396/resource_legal_interventions_to_reduce_overdose_mortality/.

WebJunction. 2018. "Opioid Crisis Responses from Public Libraries." https://www.webjunction.org/news/webjunction/opioid-resources-for-libraries.html.

Conclusion

BEING PART OF THE SOLUTION

I IMAGINE THAT FOR MOST OF US, THE IDEA OF BECOMING A librarian did not include having to be on the front line of the opioid crisis. It is a fight that we did not start, but it is one that we cannot ignore or step back from. Our communities and our patrons need libraries to support them in all areas of their lives, and this crisis is no exception. We can't afford to ignore this problem. We need to seek out members of the community affected by the opioid crisis and reach out to them and support them. By reaching out, librarians have the opportunity to make profound changes in the way people struggling with addiction are treated in society and offer them a better chance of a successful recovery.

There is an old Hawaiian parable that explains the library's efforts to change lives:

> One day, an old man was walking along a beach that was littered with thousands of starfish that had been washed ashore by the high tide. As he walked he came upon a young boy who was eagerly throwing the starfish back into the ocean, one by one.
>
> Puzzled, the man looked at the boy and asked what he was doing. Without looking up from his task, the boy simply replied, "I'm saving these starfish, Sir."

> The old man chuckled aloud, "Son, there are thousands of starfish and only one of you. What difference can you make?"
>
> The boy picked up a starfish, gently tossed it into the water and turning to the man, said, "I made a difference to that one!" (Starfish Project 2019)

Librarians can work independently or with local agencies to educate communities and individuals about the dangers of substance abuse in an effort to prevent the future use of addictive drugs. Sharing information on substance abuse prevention is simple, easy to implement, and a great way to start to collaborate with local schools, law enforcement agencies, health facilities, and other local organizations.

For patrons who are actively using the library, it's best to make the library as safe as possible for all visitors. The library can have a strong policy to guide staff on how to handle inappropriate behavior, and it can have safeguards such as a needle disposal unit, a defibrillator, and Narcan to protect visitors. Having library programs, displays, and resources readily available and promoted at the library will let people know that it is a welcoming space for people with a substance use disorder and their loved ones.

It is sad to contemplate the toll that drugs have taken on so many members of our communities, but this makes it even more critical that we try and support those people who in many ways need us the most. Being able to help people with a substance use disorder in their pursuit of recovery can become as gratifying as the ways we help shape people's everyday lives by our traditional services. The small changes in attitude that we can engineer and the opportunities for change that we create can have a profound effect on our communities, and may even save someone's life. Do whatever you can and never give up; the people in your community need your help.

REFERENCE

Starfish Project. 2019. https://starfishproject.com/the-parable/.

APPENDIX **A**

Observable Signs of Common Drugs

It is helpful to know the signs and symptoms associated with specific drugs in order to better identify, observe, and (hopefully) assist patrons who are using these substances. With that in mind, this appendix is a short guide that describes the most commonly abused substances and lists the observable signs of their use that you may encounter in the library.

Knowing some of the signs of drug use can be helpful when you come across people exhibiting symptoms. It is not important to know all the possible signs associated with all the available drugs, but it is good to have a basic understanding of what the signs of commonly abused drugs can be. Just having this information in the back of your mind can be helpful when you are around the public. For more quick information, check out some of the series on drug use that many libraries have in the children's or young adult collections. These collections, while not the most engaging reads, are a quick way for children and young adults to be introduced to these subjects and gather more specific information. These series are also helpful for adults who want information on a specific type of substance but have difficulty understanding more complex materials. Another print resource is Cynthia Kuhn and colleagues' *Buzzed: The Straight Facts about the Most Used and Abused Drugs from Alcohol to Ecstasy* (5th edition, 2019), which has been updated several times as drug use trends have changed.

You should also try to stay informed by reading news articles about new drug trends because people's drug preferences can change quickly. If you're uncertain which drugs are widely used in your community, reach out to your local law enforcement agency.

Opiates and Opioids

Opiates and opioids are all drugs known as "narcotics." They are used to block or relieve pain, and they also dull the senses and tend to induce a euphoria or "high." At higher doses the drugs produce stupor and induce sleep, and at still higher doses (overdoses) they can cause death. All of the opiates and opioids are addictive to one degree or another (U.S. National Library of Medicine 2019).

Opiates are drugs derived from opium, which comes from the poppy plant. The principal opiates are heroin, morphine, and codeine. Heroin has a long history of illegal use in the United States and has caused severe social problems in many localities. Opioids have the same effects as opiates but are synthetic. The principal opioid is oxycodone, which is marketed under the trade name OxyContin and many others. Another major opioid is fentanyl, an extremely powerful and dangerous drug. Heroin and other opiates are usually injected, while OxyContin and other opioids are usually taken in pill form. Heroin has long been illegal, but oxycodone is widely prescribed—and overprescribed—for pain relief (Center on Addiction 2017).

OPIUM

Opium is a natural substance obtained from the seed pods of the poppy plant. It has a history of use in Asia going back for centuries. Opium is moderately addictive and is usually smoked, though it can also be injected or taken in pill form. The drug is frequently combined with other drugs (DEA 2017, 46). Opium has largely been supplanted by its stronger derivatives: heroin, which is widely used illegally; and morphine, which is still used in medical settings to treat severe pain.

MORPHINE

Morphine is derived from opium and is more addictive than that compound (Editors of Encyclopaedia Britannica 2018b). Morphine is typically used by injection, but it can also be swallowed. Injection is often the preferred method because it affects the person faster. The drug is known for being a powerful pain medication and has a long association with addiction in American history.

The observable effects of morphine include:

- Confusion
- Dizziness
- Itchy skin
- Extreme drowsiness
- Pinpoint pupils
- Difficulty breathing (or inability to breathe)
- Loss of consciousness
- Weak pulse/poor circulation
- Gastrointestinal disturbances
- Nausea and vomiting

- Cyanosis or blue tint to lips and fingernails
- Coma and death in overdose situations

(Lautieri 2018)

HEROIN

Heroin is an even stronger and more addictive opiate that is made from morphine (Editors of Encyclopaedia Britannica 2018a). It is typically a white or brown powder or a black sticky substance that can be injected, smoked, or snorted (Patterson 2018a). When injected, heroin produces a powerful "rush" or high, followed by several hours of less intense feelings of well-being. Heroin is one of the most dangerously addictive of all drugs. Persons addicted to heroin experience severe withdrawal symptoms when they stop taking the drug (Editors of Encyclopaedia Britannica 2018a). Heroin was made illegal in the United States in 1924, but this did not prevent the drug from being imported illegally in large quantities starting in the late 1940s (Aviary Recovery Center 2016). Heroin addiction, with its attendant effects of crime, underground trafficking, and overdose, has devastated the populations of certain localities for decades. Heroin is often cut with other drugs or substances, some deadly and some benign. The mixing of heroin with fentanyl has become a major concern because it greatly increases the chances of an accidental overdose.

The observable effects of heroin include:

- Euphoria
- Extreme relaxation
- Drowsiness
- Sedation
- Lethargy
- Nausea and vomiting
- Grogginess
- Confusion
- Itchy skin
- Miotic or constricted pupils
- Light sensitivity
- Cyanotic (bluish) hands, feet, lips
- Decreased dental health marked by damaged teeth and swollen gums
- Excoriated skin from scratching
- Weakness and sedation

(Patterson 2018b)

The observable effects of heroin withdrawal include:

- Restlessness and discomfort
- Anxiety
- Shaking
- Sweating
- Shivering
- Pain/aches in the muscles and bones
- Vomiting

(Patterson 2018b)

OXYCODONE

Oxycodone is an opioid pain medication that is widely overprescribed and misused. It is marketed under the trade names OxyContin, Percocet, Roxicodone, Percodan, Xtampza ER, and many others. Many people start out taking the prescribed dosage of oxycodone, but as their body develops a tolerance to the drug, they find they need to increase the dosage in order to continue to feel the drug's effects—either relief from pain or a high, or both. This leads directly to addiction. Oxycodone is available in tablet or capsule form and is sometimes combined with other drugs such as aspirin or acetaminophen. The drug is usually taken orally but can also be sniffed, inhaled, or injected.

The observable effects of oxycodone use include:

- Euphoria
- Extreme relaxation
- Reduced anxiety
- Slow speech and movements
- Pain relief
- Sedation
- Nausea
- Vomiting
- Dry mouth
- Dizziness
- Drowsiness
- Flushing
- Sweating
- Weakness
- Mood changes
- Chest pain

- Hives, itching, or rash
- Swelling of the face, throat, tongue, lips, eyes, hands, feet, ankles, or lower legs
- Hoarseness
- Difficulty breathing or swallowing
- Seizures

(Brande 2018)

FENTANYL

Fentanyl is a powerful synthetic opioid that is used for breakthrough pain after surgery and for cancer pain. It is 80–100 times more potent than morphine, and many times more potent than even heroin. Because fentanyl is so potent, even small amounts of the drug are effective, and similarly, these amounts can cause overdoses and death. Tiny amounts of fentanyl are often mixed with other drugs like heroin or cocaine. The drug's strength has led to a dramatic spike in the number of deaths by overdose (DEA 2018a). Prescription fentanyl is available in the form of pills, lozenges, tablets, nasal or oral sprays, as an injectable, and as a transdermal patch (DEA 2017, 40).

The observable signs of fentanyl use include:

- Confusion
- Convulsions
- Labored breathing
- Fainting
- Dizziness or light-headedness
- A cough
- Mood changes
- Pale skin
- Nervousness
- Ulcers, sores, or white spots in the mouth
- Sneezing, sore throat, or sunken eyes
- Swelling in the calves, ankles, feet, or hands
- Fatigue
- Problems walking and balancing
- Clumsiness
- Muscle jerking or twitching
- Less responsiveness to stimuli
- Hallucinations (visual, auditory, and tactile)

- Extreme sleepiness
- Slow speech and movement
- Trembling
- Seizures

(American Addiction Centers 2018)

Withdrawing from fentanyl use is not recommended without medical assistance because of the severity of the withdrawal symptoms. The observable signs of fentanyl withdrawal include:

- Restlessness
- Yawning
- Chills
- Irritability or anxiety
- Runny nose or watery eyes
- Sweating or chills
- Overall weakness
- Widened pupils
- Rapid breathing
- Nausea
- Vomiting

(American Addiction Centers 2018)

METHADONE

Methadone is a synthetic opioid that is used to treat "opioid use disorder," that is, addiction to heroin, morphine, and other opioids. Methadone reduces the user's craving for heroin, blocks the "high" associated with the drug, and greatly reduces withdrawal symptoms. Methadone is thus uniquely suited for treating heroin dependence and has been a mainstay of opioid treatment programs for many decades. Methadone is used on a short-term basis to detoxify heroin users without causing withdrawal symptoms and is used for longer periods of time as a maintenance drug that enables people in recovery to avoid relapsing (i.e., starting to use heroin again). Methadone has enabled countless numbers of people in recovery from heroin use to recover and lead more stable, fulfilling, and productive lives (Editors of Encyclopaedia Britannica 2019a). Methadone is available in tablet, oral solution, or liquid form that can be injected or swallowed (DEA 2017, 44).

Stimulants

Stimulants increase energy and alertness and combat fatigue. They can also make people feel euphoric. The most commonly prescribed stimulants are amphetamines, which are marketed under trade names like Adderall, Ritalin, Concerta, and Dexedrine. These drugs are commonly used to treat ADHD (attention deficit hyperactivity disorder), but they are also used by people to stay awake, as study aids, and as diet pills, since the drugs suppress the appetite. A related class of drugs, methamphetamines, are similar to amphetamines but are more potent and take effect more quickly, leading to a more intense high. They are much more addictive than amphetamines, and hence are widely used illegally. Amphetamines are usually taken in pill form, while methamphetamine (or "meth") is usually taken in powder form and can be smoked, snorted (inhaled through the nose), or injected. When the stimulating effects of these drugs wear off, they are often followed by feelings of depression, lack of energy, and a washed-out feeling; this leads users to take the drugs again in order to regain the high energy level they had experienced. This repeated use, in turn, leads to addiction (Editors of Encyclopaedia Britannica 2019d; DEA 2017, 48–49).

Another common stimulant is cocaine, which is obtained from the leaves of the coca plant of South America. This drug produces a relatively short-lived euphoria that typically lasts for thirty minutes to an hour. In powder form cocaine is usually snorted (inhaled through the nose), though it can also be smoked or injected. Cocaine can be highly addictive. The crystal form of cocaine is called "crack." This drug is typically heated and smoked, and it produces an intense but very short-lived high that lasts for no more than fifteen minutes. Crack is an intensely addictive drug (Editors of Encyclopaedia Britannica 2019a).

AMPHETAMINES

Amphetamines are mainly legally prescribed and are used to treat ADHD and as diet pills. They were first used to treat nasal congestion in the 1930s, and by 1937 they were also being used to treat narcolepsy and ADHD. Amphetamines are commonly taken in pill or powder form and are taken orally.

The observable signs of amphetamine use include:

- Quicker reaction times
- Feelings of energy/wakefulness
- Excitement
- Increased attentiveness and concentration
- Feelings of euphoria
- Dry mouth
- Hostility
- Nausea
- Cognitive impairment
- Severe anxiety

- Teeth grinding
- Dizziness
- Rapid breathing rate

(Condron 2016)

METHAMPHETAMINES

Methamphetamine is a highly addictive stimulant. It is marketed under the trade name Desoxyn but is manufactured far more widely on an illegal basis in makeshift labs ("meth labs"). The drug is widely known as "meth" or "speed," and its crystalline form is called "crystal meth" (Editors of Encyclopaedia Britannica 2019c). Methamphetamine induces a powerful surge in energy and alertness that usually lasts for six to eight hours. After the drug wears off, the user "crashes" and experiences depression and fatigue, thereby leading to reuse and eventual addiction. Meth is made illegally by Mexican drug trafficking organizations and by small groups or individuals in the United States. The different precursor chemicals from which the drug is made are incredibly cheap and were formerly readily available ingredients. This is why the Combat Methamphetamine Epidemic Act of 2005 made it harder to obtain the precursor chemicals needed to make the drug—chiefly ephedrine and pseudoephedrine, which are used in over-the-counter cold and flu medications. Some retailers that sell medications containing these chemicals are now required to keep them in locked cabinets and require identification (DEA 2017, 54).

Steve Preisler, a chemist in Wisconsin, published the book *The Secrets of Methamphetamine Manufacture* in 1984. This work, which is basically a crystal meth cookbook, has now gone through several editions and is still available on Amazon.com. After the book was published, home meth labs began appearing throughout the country (Perritano 2017c, 23–28). Legislation and law enforcement efforts suppressed most of these domestic meth labs, so now the drug's manufacture is concentrated in Mexico, from where it is smuggled over the border into the United States. Methamphetamine usually comes in a powder form, and crystal meth looks like pieces of glass fragments or blue-white rocks. Methamphetamine is usually snorted, though it is also smoked or injected (DEA 2017, 54).

The observable signs of methamphetamine use include:

- Heightened energy
- Heightened awareness (feeling alert)
- Aggression
- Hyperactivity
- Rapid weight loss
- Marked malnutrition and, in severe cases, starvation

- Development of amphetamine psychosis
- Central nervous system hyperactivity and muscle tics
- Formication, or the feeling of bugs crawling under the skin, which can cause users to scratch the skin off or to create lesions that may become infected
- Deterioration of oral health ("meth mouth")
- Inflammation or infection at the site of injection, if used intravenously
- Hair loss
- Increased risk of obsessive behavior
- Reduced inhibitions, which can result in accidents and bodily harm

(Patterson 2017)

COCAINE AND CRACK

Cocaine is derived from the leaves of the coca plant and has been used for centuries by indigenous South Americans because of the euphoria and heightened energy experienced by users. In the 1970s and 1980s the drug became popular among the wealthy because it was relatively expensive. Soon, to lower the price, dealers began using baking soda or sodium hydroxide to change the powder into a crystal form (known as "rock") called crack. Crack is stronger and much more addictive than cocaine (Perritano 2013c, 38–40). Crack offers a short but very intense "high" to users that last only a few minutes. Cocaine's effects are milder and last for a half-hour to an hour.

Cocaine is commonly available as a white powder that is usually snorted. Crack is usually smoked alone or with other drugs (DEA 2017, 51).

The observable signs of cocaine use include:

- Euphoria
- Increased alertness
- Feelings of restlessness
- Irritability and anxiety
- Panic
- Paranoia
- Tremors
- Muscle twitches or tics
- Dizziness
- Dilated pupils
- Chronic, extreme fatigue

- Runny/bloody nose
- Cardiac arrest
- Stroke
- Seizures
- Respiratory arrest

    (Patterson 2018)

The observable signs of crack cocaine use include:

- Euphoria
- Increased alertness
- Excited state
- Dilated (enlarged) pupils
- Irritability
- Anxiety
- Aggressive, paranoid behavior
- Sudden death due to heart attack or stroke

    (MacLaren 2016)

Depressants

Depressants are commonly prescribed to induce sleep, treat anxiety, treat muscle spasms, and prevent seizures. They are called "depressants" because they slow down (or depress) stimulation levels in the brain, thereby inducing calm, allaying anxiety, and producing a mild euphoria. The major classes of depressants are barbiturates ("sleeping pills") and benzodiazepines ("minor tranquillizers"). The commonest and most widely used depressant, however, is alcohol. Alcohol is consumed as a liquid, and the other depressants are usually taken in pill form.

All depressants produce a sense of relaxation and a reduction in anxiety. The person's ability to retain information and memory of events while using the drugs may be impaired. These drugs can be dangerous when combined with other sedatives such as alcohol or opiates (Kuhn, Swartzwelder, and Wilson 2014, 330–31).

BARBITURATES

Aside from alcohol, barbiturates are the oldest types of depressants and were initially sold by the Bayer Company as a sleep aid. With the increase in their use, doctors became aware of these drugs' addictive properties, and moreover, it was realized that an overdose could depress the central nervous system to the point of death. Barbiturates have been replaced as sleeping aids by safer drugs, and so now they are only prescribed to prevent seizures (DEA 2017, 58). Common barbiturates include phenobarbital, pentobarbital, secobarbital, and amobarbital (Kuhn, Swartzwelder, and Wilson 2014, 329). Barbiturates are available in multicolored pills or in liquid form that can be taken orally or injected (DEA 2017, 58).

The observable signs of barbiturate use include:

- Feelings of well-being or euphoria
- Reduced inhibitions
- Relaxation
- Sleepiness and sedation
- Lethargy and unconsciousness in higher doses
- Decreased anxiety
- Insomnia
- Increased sensitivity to sound
- Increased sensitivity to pain
- Increased perspiration
- Irritability
- Hallucinations or psychosis (rare)
- Paranoia
- Memory and attention impairments
- Emotional instability
- Suicidal ideation
- Incoordination and impaired balance
- Slurred speech

  (Hatfield 2017)

The observable signs of barbiturate withdrawal include:

- Insomnia
- Rebound anxiety
- Involuntary muscle-twitching
- Excessive sweating
- Tremors
- Muscle weakness that is progressive
- Dizziness
- Nausea
- Vomiting
- Seizures
- Delirium, hallucinations, or major psychotic episodes

  (Hatfield 2017)

BENZODIAZEPINES

Benzodiazepines were synthesized starting in the 1950s because of the need for drugs that had the tranquillizing and sleep-inducing effects of barbiturates without the side effect of impaired breathing and the danger of fatal overdoses (Poole 2017a). Since the commercial introduction of Librium in 1960 and Valium in 1963, the benzodiazepines have become some of the most widely prescribed drugs in the world (Hanson 2005). Other widely used varieties are marketed under the trade names Klonopin, Ativan, and Xanax (Kuhn, Swartzwelder, and Wilson 2014, 329). Benzodiazepines are used chiefly to relieve anxiety and to treat insomnia. The drugs are also useful in treating muscle spasms and can reduce seizures. The drugs are commonly available in pill, syrup, and liquid forms and are widely misused in pill form taken orally or crushed and snorted (DEA 2017, 59).

The observable signs of benzodiazepine use include:

- Relaxation
- Decreased anxiety
- Drowsiness
- Dizziness
- Slurred speech
- Impaired coordination
- Tremors
- Nausea
- Vomiting
- Memory and cognition problems
- Confusion
- Mood swings
- Jaundice (yellowing of eyes and skin)
- Seizures
- Severe itching

  (Walker 2016)

The observable signs of benzodiazepine withdrawal include:

- Tremors
- Excessive sweating
- Difficulty concentrating
- Nausea or vomiting
- Extreme anxiety
- Insomnia
- Hallucinations

- Seizures
- Depression

(Walker 2016)

ROHYPNOL

Rohypnol is a potent benzodiazepine that reduces anxiety, relaxes muscles, and can produce a euphoric effect. The drug is not used for medical purposes in the United States but is used in other countries to treat insomnia. Rohypnol has been associated with date rape because in higher doses it can cause loss of muscle control, loss of inhibitions, amnesia, and sedation. The drug was originally made as a white pill that was odorless and tasteless, making it easy to slip into someone's drink. In 1997 the drug's manufacturer responded to these concerns by giving the pill a distinctive shape and color, and adding a dye to it so that when dissolved in a drink, it turns the liquid blue. Generic versions of the pill may not contain the dye (DEA 2017, 62).

GHB

Gamma-hydroxybutyric acid (GHB) is a depressant and sedative that is well known as a date rape drug. When in liquid form the drug is clear and colorless, and has a slightly salty taste. The drug has euphoric and calming effects and is misused against others because it increases libido, passivity, and suggestibility, and causes amnesia (DEA 2017, 60–61).

ALCOHOL

Alcohol is a legal drug, but one that is important to discuss because of the behavioral issues and dangers associated with intoxication and detoxification. Because of the high percentage of people who consume alcohol, intoxicated behavior is a common concern for libraries.

Alcohol is a depressant, meaning that it slows down body functions. It makes people feel more relaxed and socially outgoing. Negatively, it can impair muscular coordination, interfere with decision-making, and cause a gap in response times, making it a very common cause of automobile accidents. Consuming large amounts of alcohol can seriously interfere with muscle coordination, making it more difficult for someone to control their balance and bodily movements. Alcohol can also dull the body's responses to touch and pain, so that an intoxicated person who is injured may either be unaware of the injury or not aware that the injury requires medical attention. An additional risk is when alcohol is consumed along with other sedatives (opiates, barbiturates, benzodiazepines, and cold medicines) because this can cause unconsciousness, breathing problems, or even death (Kuhn, Swartzwelder, Wilson 2014, 30–31).

The observable signs of alcohol use include:

- Slowed reaction times and reflexes
- Poor motor coordination
- Slurred speech
- Lowered inhibitions and increase in risk behavior
- Lowered reasoning ability, impaired judgment
- Confusion, anxiety, restlessness
- Slowed breathing rate
- Heavy sweating
- Nausea and vomiting
- Coma
- The smell of alcohol on breath or clothing
- Loss of consciousness

(Center for Substance Abuse Research 2013a)

The light, moderate, or occasional consumption of alcohol is relatively harmless and does not lead to dependence. Moreover, alcohol can lead to addiction (alcoholism) in some people but not in many others. It all depends on the individual. The withdrawal symptoms experienced when a person stops drinking can be mild to serious, depending on how long the person has consumed alcohol and the amount of alcohol typically consumed each day. People who have been drinking heavily for weeks, months, or years typically experience serious withdrawal symptoms when they stop drinking.

The withdrawal symptoms of alcoholism include:

- Anxiety or nervousness
- Depression
- Fatigue
- Irritability
- Jumpiness or shakiness
- Mood swings
- Nightmares
- Not thinking clearly
- Sweating, clammy skin
- Enlarged (dilated) pupils
- Headache
- Insomnia
- Nausea and vomiting
- Tremor of the hands or other body parts

A severe form of alcohol withdrawal called delirium tremens can cause:
- Agitation
- Fever
- Seeing or feeling things that aren't there (hallucinations)
- Seizures
- Severe confusion

(U.S. National Library of Medicine 2017)

Hallucinogens

Hallucinogens are drugs that cause people to experience an altered sense of reality. A person taking a hallucinogen may see, hear, or feel things that are not real or that are distorted (i.e., hallucinations). Drugs that alter perception and produce hallucinations are also known as "psychedelics" due to their close association with the "psychedelic" youth counterculture of the 1960s. Some types of hallucinogens are obtained from plants and mushrooms, while other types are chemically synthesized in the laboratory. The hallucinogens obtained from natural sources have an incredibly long history of religious and mystical use by many cultures.

Hallucinogenic drugs are divided into two main categories: the classical hallucinogens, which produce hallucinations; and deliriant and dissociative drugs, which, in addition to hallucinations, cause a detachment from reality in which users feel they are unreal or are disconnected from themselves, or experience the world itself as unreal. The classical hallucinogens are LSD, psilocybin, peyote (mescaline), and DMT. The chief deliriants and dissociatives are PCP (phencyclidine) and ketamine (Gonzales 2018). There are two other important drugs that are sometimes classed as hallucinogens: marijuana and ecstasy (MDMA). Marijuana is used extremely widely and has recently become legal in some U.S. states. This drug produces perceptual distortions that are characteristic of the hallucinogens, but it also has certain effects that are common to stimulants and depressants. Ecstasy imparts increased energy and altered sensations, and thus has both stimulant and hallucinogenic effects.

It is not known exactly how the classical hallucinogens affect the mind and body, but most research suggests that these drugs affect the serotonin receptors in the brain. These receptors are located throughout the brain, which is why the drugs may affect multiple senses. In some cases hallucinogens can be addictive. Although they can have a powerful perceptual impact on people, users do not typically become dependent on the drugs and crave them (National Institute on Drug Abuse 2019a). Deaths from overdoses are also rare, but in some cases a person is killed or injured from an accident (such as falling through a window) because of their altered state of reality (*Psychology Today* 2019).

The drug descriptions in this section will start with two of the classical hallucinogens (LSD and psilocybin), then treat the dissociatives and deliriants (PCP and ketamine), and conclude with descriptions of marijuana and ecstasy.

LSD

LSD (lysergic acid diethylamide) is one of the better-known hallucinogens. LSD is made from lysergic acid, a chemical compound present in the ergot fungus, which grows on rye and other cereal grains. LSD is a powerful hallucinogen that induces visual hallucinations and other altered perceptions, feelings, and thoughts. An LSD "trip" can last as long as twelve hours and is often stimulating and pleasurable, but it can also turn negative and generate intense feelings of anxiety, panic, and paranoia, in which case it is termed a "bad trip" (Alcohol and Drug Foundation 2019). LSD is usually taken orally as a pill, caplet, or tablet, or on blotting paper (DEA 2017, 70).

The observable signs of LSD use include:

- Hallucinations
- Intense sensory experiences
- Dilated pupils
- Salivation
- Dry mouth
- Weakness
- Tremors
- Facial flushing
- Chills and gooseflesh
- Sweating
- Nausea
- Dizziness
- Visual hallucinations
- Synesthesia—a blending of sensory perception (i.e., "hearing" colors or "seeing" sounds)
- The sense that one is undergoing a profound mystical or religious experience
- Intense anxiety
- Panic
- Delusions
- Paranoia
- Rapid mood swings
- The feeling that one is losing one's identity

- The fear that one is disintegrating into nothingness and reality does not exist
- Some users may experience seizures

    (Center for Substance Abuse Research 2013d)

PSILOCYBIN MUSHROOMS

Psilocybin mushrooms are another popular hallucinogen. The mushrooms that are most commonly used as hallucinogens are from several genera, including *Psilocybe*, *Panaeolus*, and *Conocybe*. The most widely used species of mushrooms are *Psilocybe mexicana* and *Psilocybe cyanescans* (Kuhn, Swartzwelder, and Wilson 2014, 147). The mushrooms are available dried or in various other forms that can be eaten, smoked, or injected.

The observable signs of psilocybin mushroom use include:

- Hallucinations (most often visual but can occur in any sensory domain)
- Intense emotions and sensory experiences
- Synesthesia
- Changes in perception of time
- Psychological regression to earlier experiences/states
- Impaired judgment and potential for harm or death due to accidents
- Paranoia
- Psychosis
- Severe anxiety that may manifest as panic attacks
- Increased risk of having a "bad trip," which may be emotionally disturbing
- Excessive sweating
- Dilated pupils
- Irregular breathing
- Tremors
- Coordination problems
- Dry mouth

    (Hatfield 2018)

PCP

PCP (phencyclidine), also known as "angel dust," causes hallucinations, feelings of detachment from reality, and a wide spectrum of other mental effects. The drug was developed in the 1950s as an anesthetic but was not used for this purpose for very long because of the agitation, sensory distortions, and hostile behavior that it caused. Today, PCP is a recreational drug that is typically smoked (sometimes mixed with tobacco or marijuana), though it is also taken by mouth, snorted, or injected (Perritano 2017a, 46). PCP is dangerous because in addition to its more benign effects it can cause irrational, violent, and even psychotic behavior (Kuhn, Swartzwelder, and Wilson 2014, 161). The drug is also addictive, and withdrawal from it must usually be undertaken in a hospital setting.

The observable signs of PCP use include:

- Mild to intense euphoria
- Relaxation or drowsiness
- Feelings of unreality and dissociation with the environment
- Distorted sense of one's body, including a feeling of weightlessness
- Distorted sense of time and space
- Visual and auditory hallucinations and other sensory distortions
- Difficulty concentrating and thinking
- Anxiety
- Agitation
- Paranoid thoughts
- Confusion and disorientation
- Intense feelings of alienation
- Bizarre or hostile behavior
- Obsession with trivial matters
- Grandiose delusions
- Panic, terror, and an overwhelming fear of imminent death
- Impaired motor skills
- Blurred vision and constricted pupils
- Dizziness
- Painful reaction to sound
- Blank staring
- Speech disturbances, ranging from difficulty articulating to incoherent speech or inability to speak
- Muscular rigidity

- Decreased sensitivity or awareness of pain, touch, and position
- Stupor or coma
- Slow, shallow, and irregular breathing
- Nausea/vomiting
- Increased body temperature and sweating alternating with chills and shivering
- Very high doses may result in an overdose and lead to coma, convulsions, or death

(Center for Substance Abuse Research 2013f)

KETAMINE

Calvin Stevens developed ketamine in an attempt to replace PCP with another anesthetic for use in the Vietnam War. Ketamine is still used in medical and veterinary settings but has also become a popular party drug. It has both psychedelic properties and strong anesthetic properties that will make people go into a trancelike state (Perritano 2017a, 50–51). Ketamine is often called a date rape drug because it can be added to the drinks of unaware individuals. Ketamine is dangerous because it impairs a person's ability to register pain, so that someone may become seriously injured and not register that medical assistance is needed. Ketamine is available in a liquid or powder and is snorted, smoked, mixed into drinks, and is often combined with other drugs (DEA 2017, 68).

The observable signs of ketamine use include:

- Slowed or difficult breathing
- Impaired ability to think
- Amnesia
- Impaired motor functioning
- Delirium (hallucinations or disorientation)
- The dramatic increase in heart rate (tachycardia)
- Loss of touch with reality (de-realization)
- Loss of coordination
- Sense of invulnerability
- Muscle rigidity
- Aggressive/violent behavior

(Center for Substance Abuse Research 2013c)

MARIJUANA

Marijuana is the third most widely used recreational drug in the United States, after alcohol and tobacco (Northwest Indiana Times 2019). As of early 2020, it was completely legal in eleven states and was legal for medical use in almost all the rest of the states (Berke and Gould 2020). Marijuana consists of the dried flowers, buds, and leaves of the plant *Cannabis sativa*, from which the drug gets its alternate name, "cannabis." These plant parts contain the psychoactive ingredient in marijuana, THC (tetrahydrocannabinol). Marijuana is a hallucinogen of mild to moderate strength that also has stimulant and depressant properties, hence its ambiguous taxonomic status (National Institute on Drug Abuse 2019b).

Marijuana is typically smoked, though it can also be ingested orally. The drug produces euphoria, altered perceptions, heightened mood, and increased appetite, and at higher doses, it causes sensory illusions and hallucinations. Upon being smoked, marijuana takes effect almost immediately, and the high last anywhere from two to four hours. When ingested orally, it takes effect in thirty to sixty minutes. Marijuana has certain medical uses, chiefly to suppress nausea and vomiting during chemotherapy. The negative health effects of prolonged marijuana use are unclear (Jannetto 2020).

The observable signs of marijuana use include:

- Dizziness or trouble walking
- Red, bloodshot, or glazed eyes
- Smell of marijuana

(Center for Substance Abuse Research 2013g)

ECSTASY

Ecstasy (MDMA) is a derivative of methamphetamine that causes hallucinations, among other effects. The German company Merck first synthesized MDMA in 1912 as a drug to prevent abnormal bleeding. MDMA was never commonly used, however, until Alexander Shulgin, a U.S. chemist and psychopharmacologist, published research in the 1970s showing the drug's psychoactive effects. MDMA then came into limited use to help psychologists treat patients with various mental health issues. The drug was found to produce a pleasurable, affectionate, and euphoric state of mind, and because it is both a stimulant and a hallucinogen, it became very popular with clubs and parties (Perritano 2017a, 36–37). The drug achieved considerable popularity in the 1980s under the nickname "ecstasy," by which it is now generally known. Unlike other hallucinogens, ecstasy can cause an overdose because it inhibits the body's ability to regulate temperature, so the person can overheat, damaging vital organs. The drug increases energy and focus, decreases appetite, and gives the user a warm euphoric feeling (Kuhn, Swartzwelder, and Wilson 2014, 112). The drug is commonly taken in tablet form but is also found in capsule, powder, and liquid forms (DEA 2017, 66).

The observable signs of ecstasy use include:

- Euphoria
- Heightened emotions
- Heightened sense of mental clarity
- Hallucinations
- Sweating
- Chills
- Elevated anxiety
- Nausea
- Involuntary clenching of the teeth
- Muscle tension
- Tremors
- Fainting
- Seizures

(Villa 2018)

Inhalants

An inhalant is any household or industrial chemical whose vapor is inhaled through the nose or mouth. It is not the item itself that is an issue, but the vapors from the item that can cause a person to get high. (Substances like tobacco and marijuana that are burned before being inhaled are not classified as inhalants.)

There is almost no limit to the types of inhalants that people have used to get high, but most of them can be categorized into four types of substances. *Aerosols* are liquids that are stored in pressured containers so that the liquid can be sprayed. Spray paint and hairspray are among these inhalants. *Volatile solvents* like gasoline, toluene, and paint thinner are liquids that turn to vapor very easily. Nail polish and various types of glue are also commonly used as inhalants. *Gases* are the third category and are already in the form needed for abuse; nitrous oxide (used at the dentist's office or in whipped cream cans), butane, and propane can all be misused as inhalants. The fourth class of substances are *nitrites*, which dilate blood vessels and are used as sexual enhancers (National Institute on Drug Abuse 2017).

Most inhalants (except for nitrites) slow down the central nervous system (Poole 2017a, 49–52), producing an initial "high" followed by light-headedness and drowsiness. Inhalants are dangerous and easy to overdose on.

Sudden sniffing death syndrome (SSDS) occurs when a person goes into cardiac arrest after using an inhalant. For other users, inhaling can cause seizures or damage other vital organs. The long-term use of inhalants can have cause damage to the brain and central nervous system (Poole 2017a, 55).

The observable signs of inhalant use include:

- Chemical odors from the person or their breath
- Slurred speech
- Dulled senses
- Lack of coordination
- Paint or stains on the body or clothing
- Hidden rags, clothes, or empty containers
- Spots or sores around the mouth or nose
- Red or runny eyes and nose
- A dazed or dizzy appearance
- Excitability
- Irritability
- General lack of emotion

(Center for Substance Abuse Research 2013b)

REFERENCES

Alcohol and Drug Foundation. 2019. "LSD." https://adf.org.au/drug-facts/lsd/.

American Addiction Centers. 2018. "Fentanyl Addiction: Symptoms and Signs of Abuse." October 11. https://americanaddictioncenters.org/fentanyl-treatment/signs-of-abuse.

Aviary Recovery Center. 2016. "A Timeline of the Heroin Epidemic." https://aviaryrecoverycenter.com/timeline-heroin-epidemic/

BBC News. 2017. "True Blood Star Died from Alcohol Withdrawal Complications." www.bbc.com/news/entertainment-arts-40569402.

Berke, Jeremy, and Skye Gould. 2020. "Legal Marijuana Just Went on Sale in Illinois. Here Are All the States Where Cannabis Is Legal," *Business Insider*, January 1. https://www.businessinsider.com/legal-marijuana-states-2018-1.

Brande, Lauren. 2018. "What Are the Side Effects of Oxycodone?" American Addiction Centers. August 10. https://drugabuse.com/library/the-effects-of-oxycodone-use/.

Center for Substance Abuse Research. 2013a. "Alcohol." October 31. www.cesar.umd.edu/cesar/drugs/alcohol.asp.

———. 2013b. "Inhalants." October 31. www.cesar.umd.edu/cesar/drugs/inhalants.asp.

———. 2013c. "Ketamine." October 31. www.cesar.umd.edu/cesar/drugs/ketamine.asp.

———. 2013d. "LSD." October 31. www.cesar.umd.edu/cesar/drugs/lsd.asp.

———. 2013e. "Psilocybin/Psilocyn." October 31. www.cesar.umd.edu/cesar/drugs/psilocybin.asp.

———. 2013f. "Phencyclidine (PCP)." October 31. www.cesar.umd.edu/cesar/drugs/pcp.asp.

——— 2013g. "Marijuana." October 29. http://www.cesar.umd.edu/cesar/drugs/marijuana.asp

Center on Addiction. 2017. "We Asked, You Answered: Is There a Difference Between an Opioid and an Opiate?" September 28. https://www.centeronaddiction.org/the-buzz-blog/we-asked-you-answered-there-difference-between-opioid-and-opiate.

Condron, Patrick. 2016. "The Effects of Amphetamine Use." American Addiction Centers. December 28. https://drugabuse.com/library/the-effects-of-amphetamine-use/.

DEA Drug Enforcement Administration. 2017. *Drugs of Abuse: A DEA Resource Guide, 2017 Edition*. www.dea.gov/sites/default/files/sites/getsmartaboutdrugs.com/files/publications/DoA_2017Ed_Updated_6.16.17.pdf.

———. 2018a. "Fentanyl." www.dea.gov/factsheets/fentanyl.

———. 2018b. "Justice Department, DEA Propose Significant Opioid Manufacturing Reduction in 2019." www.dea.gov/press-releases/2018/08/16/justice-department-dea-propose-significant-opioid-manufacturing-reduction.

The Editors of Encyclopaedia Britannica. 2018a. "Heroin." Encyclopaedia Britannica. https://www.britannica.com/science/heroin.

———. 2018b. "Opium." Encyclopaedia Britannica. https://www.britannica.com/science/opium.

———. 2019a. "Cocaine." Encyclopaedia Britannica. https://www.britannica.com/science/cocaine.

———. 2019b. "Methadone." Encyclopaedia Britannica. https://www.britannica.com/science/methadone.

———. 2019c. "Methamphetamine." Encyclopaedia Britannica. https://www.britannica.com/science/methamphetamine.

———. 2019d. "Stimulant." Encyclopaedia Britannica. https://www.britannica.com/science/stimulant.

Gonzales, Matt. 2018. "Hallucinogen Abuse." DrugRehab. https://www.drugrehab.com/addiction/drugs/hallucinogens/.

Hanson, David J. 2005. "Librium." Chemical and Engineering News 83, no. 24 (June). https://cen.acs.org/articles/83/i25/Librium.html.

Hatfield, Rudolph. 2017. "Barbiturates' Side Effects." American Addiction Centers, October 24. https://drugabuse.com/library/barbiturates-side-effects/.

———. 2018. "The Effects of Psilocybin Use." American Addiction Centers, March 1. https://drugabuse.com/library/effects-psilocybin-mushrooms/.

Jannetto, Paul J. 2020. "Cannabis." In *Clinical Toxicology Testing: A Guide for Laboratory Professionals*, 2nd ed., edited by Barbarajean Magnami, Tai C. Kwong, Gwendolyn A. McMillin, and Alan H. B. Wu. Northfield, IL: College of American Pathologists, 2020, 205–13. http://elss.cap.orgelss/ShowProperty?nodePath=/UCMCON/Contribution%20Folders/WebApplications/pdf/Tox2_Sample Pages.pdf.

Kuhn, Cynthia, Scott Swartzwelder, and Wilkie Wilson. 2014. *Buzzed: The Straight Facts about the Most Used and Abused Drugs from Alcohol to Ecstasy*. 4th ed. New York: W. W. Norton.

Lautieri, Amanda 2018. "Morphine Abuse." American Addiction Centers. https://drugabuse.com/library/morphine-abuse/.

MacLaren, Erik. 2016. "The Effects of Crack Use." American Addiction Centers. December 20. https://drugabuse.com/library/the-effects-of-crack-use/.

National Institute on Drug Abuse. 2017. "Inhalants." https://www.drugabuse.gov/publications/drugfacts/inhalants.

———. 2019a. "Hallucinogens." https://www.drugabuse.gov/publications/drugfacts/hallucinogens.

———. 2019b. "Marijuana." https://www.drugabuse.gov/publications/drugfacts/marijuana.

Northwest Indiana Times. 2019. "25 Most Commonly Used Recreational Drugs in America." *Get Healthy*, August 23. https://www.nwitimes.com/niche/get-healthy/most-commonly-used-recreational-drugs-in-america/collection_b0f525bd-4a79-5e72-961a-87be6edf2460.html#1.

Patterson, Eric. 2017. "The Effects of Meth Use." American Addiction Centers. October 27. https://drugabuse.com/library/the-effects-of-meth-use/.

———. 2018a. "The Effects of Cocaine Use." American Addiction Centers. September 5. https://drugabuse.com/library/the-effects-of-cocaine-use/.

———. 2018b. "The Effects of Heroin Use." American Addiction Centers. January 30. https://drugabuse.com/library/the-effects-of-heroin-use/.

———. 2018c. "Opiate Abuse." American Addiction Centers. https://drugabuse.com/library/opiate-abuse/.

Perritano, John. 2017a. *Hallucinogens: Ecstasy, LSD, and Ketamine*. Broomall, PA: Mason Crest.

———. 2017b. *Opioids: Heroin, OxyContin, and Painkillers*. Broomall, PA: Mason Crest.

———. 2017c. *Stimulants: Meth, Cocaine, and Amphetamines*. Broomall, PA: Mason Crest.

Poole, H. W. 2017a. *Alcohol and Tobacco*. Broomall, PA: Mason Crest.

———. 2017b. *Over-the-Counter Drugs*. Broomall, PA: Mason Crest.

———. 2017c. *Prescription Drugs*. Broomall, PA: Mason Crest.

Psychology Today. 2019. "Hallucinogens." https://www.psychologytoday.com/us/conditions/hallucinogens.

U.S. National Library of Medicine. 2017. "Alcohol Withdrawal." MedlinePlus. January 14. https://medlineplus.gov/ency/article/000764.htm.

———. "Opioid Misuse and Addiction." MedlinePlus. https://medlineplus.gov/opioidmisuseandaddiction.html.

Villa, Lauren. 2018. "The Effects of Ecstasy Use." American Addiction Centers. October 1. https://drugabuse.com/library/the-effects-of-ecstasy-use/.

Walker, Leah. 2016. "The Effects of Benzodiazepine Use." American Addiction Centers. July 5. https://drugabuse.com/library/effects-benzodiazepine-use/.

APPENDIX **B**

Further Reading and Viewing

As the substance abuse crisis continues to destroy more lives, more books, films, and online resources are being produced on the topic of addiction and recovery. The following are some of the resources that I have used and that I recommend.

RECOMMENDED BOOKS FOR ADULTS

Barnett, Robin. 2016. *Addict in the House: A No-Nonsense Family Guide through Addiction and Recovery*. Oakland, CA: New Harbinger Publications.
    A straightforward introduction to addiction and how people can help someone in recovery. This book is written for families, but it is helpful for anyone who has someone struggling with addiction in their life.

Brand, Russell. 2017. *Recovery: Freedom from our Addictions*. New York: Henry Holt.
    Russell Brand's comedic relief and straight talk make this memoir/self-help book one that many will find helpful. He demonstrates that recovery is not an easy process, and that for him it is still a constant battle that he will have to wage forever.

Burnwell, D'Anne. 2015. *Saving Jake: When Addiction Hits Home*. FocusUp Books.
    Burnwell's heartbreaking memoir shares her experience of having her teenage son begin using OxyContin, which led to heroin use. This all-too-common tale is unfortunately one that many parents experience, and Burnwell's memoir and research could be helpful to other family members of people struggling with addiction.

Bydlowska, Jowita. 2014. *Drunk Mom: A Memoir*. New York: Penguin Books.
    Bydlowska was a young mother struggling with alcoholism, and unlike many other memoirs, this book was written after only one year of sobriety. The book provides a raw insight into alcoholism and those new to recovery.

Clegg, Bill. 2012. *Ninety Days: A Memoir of Recovery*. New York: Little, Brown.
> This book is the sequel to *Portrait of an Addict as a Young Man* and follows Clegg's recovery from crack. I would recommend this book to family and friends, but would be cautious in recommending it to those in recovery, since many sections of the book may be triggering. But if you know someone who is looking for a factual account of recovery, I would recommend this book.

Clegg, Bill. 2010. *Portrait of an Addict as a Young Man: A Memoir*. New York: Little, Brown.
> In this memoir Clegg talks about how his addiction to crack affected his successful business, as well as his partner, family, and friends. His addiction destroys almost everything in his life and almost kills him. Clegg's beautiful writing makes this memoir one I would highly recommend.

De Quincey, Thomas. 1971. *Confessions of an English Opium-Eater*. Harmondsworth, UK: Penguin.
> This book was originally published in 1821 and is one of the earliest memoirs of drug addiction. Thomas De Quincey was an English essayist who began using laudanum (a form of opium) in response to physical and psychological issues. His descriptions of his experiences with opium and his addiction to the drug make this account a true classic.

Foote, Jeffrey. 2014. *Beyond Addiction: How Science and Kindness Help People Change*. New York: Scribner.
> This book is written for the family and friends of people with a substance use disorder. It provides practical advice on how people can play an active role in the recovery of a loved one while also caring for themselves.

Haroutunian, Harry. 2016. *Not as Prescribed: Recognizing and Facing Alcohol and Drug Misuse in Older Adults*. Center City, MN: Hazelden.
> Most books focus on the addiction of young adults, but this book is a critical resource for those concerned about older adults. The book helps people to understand which symptoms are signs of normal aging and which are signs of addiction.

Kuhn, Cynthia, Scott Swartzwelder, and Wilkie Wilson. 2019. *Buzzed: The Straight Facts about the Most Used and Abused Drugs from Alcohol to Ecstasy*. 5th ed. New York: W. W. Norton.
> There are several editions of this highly useful reference source. The book provides information on how people use various drugs, how these drugs affect the body, the short- and long-term effects of use, and signs of possible overdose. I have used this book many times for reference professionally and have also recommended it to caregivers who suspect substance use.

Macy, Beth. 2018. *Dopesick: Dealers, Doctors, and the Drug Company That Addicted America*. New York: Little, Brown.
> Journalist Beth Macy tells the complex history of opioids in America, starting with one dealer in a small Virginia town. She shows how the opioid epidemic was fueled by both medical overtreatment and corporate greed.

Newton, David E. 2018. *The Opioid Crisis: A Reference Handbook*. Santa Barbara, CA: ABC-CLIO.

This resource provides the background and history of the opioid crisis, current problems, controversies, proposed solutions, and individual perspectives that demonstrate different points of view.

Quinones, Sam. 2015. *Dreamland: The True Tale of America's Opiate Epidemic*. New York: Bloomsbury.

This well-researched book about the opiate epidemic uses the examples of young men involved in drug trafficking and the history of Purdue Pharma to describe drug culture and addiction. There is also a young adult adaptation of this book that was published in 2019.

Reding, Nick. 2009. *Methland: The Death and Life of an American Small Town*. New York: Bloomsbury.

This moving story focuses on the small town of Oelwein, Iowa, which like so many other small towns is struggling with the easy access to methamphetamines. The book covers a four-year period focusing on the town doctor, the prosecutor, and an individual addicted to methamphetamines.

Rodriguez, Luis J. 2011. *It Calls You Back: An Odyssey through Love, Addiction, Revolutions, and Healing*. New York: Simon & Schuster.

Rodriguez's second memoir (his first is *Always Running*) talks about his life after leaving a gang, spending time in prison, and combating his addiction to heroin. This story of recovery can be inspirational for many people.

Sheff, David. 2008. *Beautiful Boy: A Father's Journey through His Son's Addiction*. Boston: Houghton Mifflin.

Journalist David Sheff's memoir is a beautifully heartfelt story about his son's addiction to methamphetamines and how this impacted him and their family. I have received great feedback from many friends and families of those struggling with addiction about how this book made them realize that they are not alone.

Sheff, David. 2013. *Clean: Overcoming America's Greatest Tragedy*. Boston: Houghton Mifflin Harcourt.

Sheff uses the research he undertook when confronted with his son's addiction to share with readers information about drug addiction, treatments for families, and solutions for the nation.

Smith, Lisa F. 2016. *Girl Walks Out of a Bar: A Memoir*. New York: SelectBooks.

This is an honest and darkly humorous memoir of a New York City lawyer who self-medicated her anxiety and depression with alcohol and drug use. She talks about her life before, during, and after addiction in a way that many people can relate to.

Sixx, Nikki. 2017. *The Heroin Diaries: A Year in the Life of a Shattered Rock Star*. New York: Gallery Books.

Nikki Sixx was known as the bassist and songwriter for Motley Crue and for living the sex, drugs, and rock-and-roll lifestyle. This memoir describes his struggle with addiction based on his journal from December 1986 to December 1987. The book also contains some drawings, photos, poetry, and song lyrics by him. While I was working in Tewksbury, this was the most popular addiction memoir for those in recovery.

Temple, John. 2015. *American Pain: How a Young Felon and His Ring of Doctors Unleashed America's Drug Epidemic*. Guilford, CT: Lyons.

This award-winning true crime book is about how the felon Chris George teamed up with a local doctor to take advantage of the under-regulated market for prescription pain medications. This book demonstrates how this relationship (and others like it) created the opioid crisis.

Wittels Wachs, Stephanie. 2018. *Everything Is Horrible and Wonderful: A Tragicomic Memoir of Genius, Heroin, Love, and Loss*. Naperville, IL: Sourcebooks.

Harris Wittels was a comedian, actor, writer, and producer known for his roles in the TV shows *Parks and Recreation* and *The Sarah Silverman Program*. He died from a heroin overdose in 2015. His sister Stephanie shares her story about her brother's addiction and her grief in the first year after his death.

RECOMMENDED BOOKS FOR YOUNG ADULTS

Goldsmith, Connie. 2018. *Addiction and Overdose: Confronting an American Crisis*. Minneapolis, MN: Twenty-First Century Books.

Though written for young adults, this book would also be very helpful for parents and teachers. It includes stories of people in recovery and from the families and friends who are grieving the loss of someone who died from an overdose. The book also includes general information about substance use disorders, how to identify the signs of addiction, and how to help someone who may be struggling with addiction.

Krosoczka, Jarrett J. 2018. *Hey, Kiddo*. New York: Graphix.

This graphic memoir written and illustrated by Jarrett Krosoczka is about growing up with his grandparents, who adopted him after his mother—who was struggling with heroin addiction—was incarcerated. The book details the young man's interactions with his mother and the impact her addiction had on his life.

Newton, David E. 2016. *Youth Substance Abuse: A Reference Handbook*. Santa Barbara, CA: ABC-CLIO.

This book is part of the Contemporary World Issues series and is a thorough reference work on substance abuse. It goes into the history of substance use, the substances commonly used, what effects and treatments are available for the use of specific substances, and individual perspectives on an assortment of topics related to substance use. The book also treats topics not covered in other sources, including the introduction of vaping and the relationship between substance abuse and transgendered youth.

Quinones, Sam. 2019. *Dreamland: The True Tale of America's Opiate Epidemic: A Young Adult Adaption*. New York: Bloomsbury.
> This book is a young adult adaptation of the adult book of the same title. It explains how the opiate epidemic originated, just as the adult title does, but it focuses on young adults affected by the crisis and includes resources and a discussion guide.

Sheff, David, and Nic Sheff. 2019. *High: Everything You Want to Know about Drugs, Alcohol, and Addiction*. Boston: Houghton Mifflin Harcourt.
> This book by a father and son is an accessible yet detailed work about drugs and addiction. It provides information on a variety of substances, why they are used, the risks of their use, and testimonials by people affected by them. There is also a chapter that discusses treatment, relapse, and recovery.

Sheff, Nic. 2007. *Tweak: Growing Up on Methamphetamines*. New York: Atheneum Books for Young Readers.
> Nic Sheff (whose father wrote the adult memoir *Beautiful Boy*) tells his story of substance abuse, which started with alcohol and led to methamphetamines. The book is about Nic's recovery, which includes relapse. The story is one of hope and success told in a heartbreakingly honest way that can have a strong impact on readers.

Sheff, Nic. 2011. *We All Fall Down: Living with Addiction*. New York: Little, Brown.
> This book is the follow-up to Nic Sheff's first book, *Tweak*, and is about his struggle with relapse and recovery. He talks openly about his recovery in rehabilitation centers and what sober living is like after recovery.

RECOMMENDED BOOKS FOR CHILDREN

Black, Claudia. 2018. *My Dad Loves Me, My Dad Has a Disease: A Child's View: Living with Addiction*. Las Vegas: Central Recovery.
> This children's book is a collection of illustrations and drawings done by children who have a family member with a substance use disorder. The book may be a comfort to children by letting them know that they are not alone in their experiences and that what they have experienced may be the result of addiction.

Bryan, Tracy. 2015. *Explaining Addiction for Kids*. Tracy Bryan.
> This book for young children explains addiction simply and in general terms without going into details on specific drugs. It is a great introduction to the concept of addiction.

Crosson, Denise D. Illustrated by Mike Motz. 2008. *Mommy's Gone to Treatment*. Las Vegas: Central Recovery.
> In this picture book a girl's mother is not home when she wakes up, and when she asks her father, he tells her that her mother is sick with an addiction and has gone to the hospital for treatment. The father explains the signs that her mother was sick and why she needs help. Father and daughter visit the mother in treatment when she is able to have visitors. The book includes a resource guide for parents.

Heegaard, Marge. 1996. *When a Family Is in Trouble: Children Can Cope with Grief from Drug and Alcohol Addiction*. Minneapolis, MN: Woodland Press.
> This interactive workbook is an excellent tool for professionals and families to use with children. The book helps children understand what a problem in the family might be like, what addiction is, how the child might feel about addiction, and how to handle those emotions, problem-solving, and self-care.

Moore, Helen H. Illustrated by John Blackford. 2010. *The Secret History of Willow Ridge: Gabe's Dad Finds Recovery*. Las Vegas: Central Recovery.
> This chapter book is about 10-year-old Gabe, his 7-year-old sister Izzy, and their father, who is struggling with a substance use disorder. The book is about what it might be like to live with someone who has an addiction, and what the treatment processes might be like.

O'Flaherty, Johanna, and Hortensia DeJesus. Illustrated by Safar Lina. 2015. *Daddy Goes to Meetings*. Las Vegas, NV: Central Recovery.
> This picture book for children is an introduction to outpatient addiction treatment. The book tells the story of a father who is struggling with addiction, how that impacts the family, and then how, with the help of friends, the father is convinced to attend meetings. The mother and children sometimes visit during the meetings. The end of the book includes a guide for parents.

Palmore, Elaine Mitchell. Illustrated by Norris Hall. 2011. *The Dragon Who Lives at Our House*. Minneapolis, MN: Rising Star Studios.
> In this children's picture book, a dragon is used to represent a father's addiction. The dragon becomes more disruptive to the family's life, resulting in a temporary separation, with the father going into recovery and managing the dragon. This book was recommended to me by law enforcement officials who found it helpful in their work with children.

RECOMMENDED FILMS AND TELEVISION PROGRAMS ON ADDICTION

Addiction. 2012. HBO Documentary Films.
> This fourteen-part documentary series includes online resources to aid in a discussion for people after watching the film. The documentary talks about the truth of addiction versus the stereotypes and common misunderstandings about it, what causes addiction, and what treatment options are available.

Addiction. 2019. WGBH.
> This documentary interviews individuals struggling with addiction, as well as scientists and doctors on the opioid crisis. It talks about how the opioid epidemic became a national crisis, what is being and should be done to help those in need, and what changes to make in order to prevent addiction in the future.

The Anonymous People. 2014. Alive Mind Cinema.
> This documentary takes a deep look into the stigma and discrimination faced by the millions of Americans who are recovering from an addiction. It talks about current recovery options and the need for increased services for people to enter and maintain recovery. The film also talks about the impact that stigma and discrimination have on people who have a substance use disorder, and how this impacts the lives of those seeking recovery or in recovery.

Beautiful Boy. 2019. Lions Gate.
> Based on the book by the same title, this movie tells the story of David Sheff and his son Nic Sheff's struggle with addiction to methamphetamine. The movie shows how Nic's addiction impacted his and his family's lives and what his father did to save his son and his family.

Chasing Heroin. 2016. A Frontline Production with RAINmedia.
> A journalistic view on the heroin crisis and how shifting the treatment of those with an addiction from criminalization to compassion and health care is improving people's chance for recovery.

Heroin: Cape Cod, USA. 2016. HBO Documentary Films.
> This documentary focuses on the impact that heroin addiction has on individuals and their loved ones in the Cape Cod region of Massachusetts. It does an excellent job of demonstrating the impact that addiction has on a community.

Hooked: Illegal Drugs and How They Got That Way. 2008. Tera Media for the History Channel.
> This documentary series looks into the history of commonly abused drugs such as marijuana, methamphetamines, opium, morphine, heroin, cocaine, LSD, and ecstasy. Though a bit dated, the documentary does a wonderful job of explaining the long history of drugs and how societal decisions have impacted drug usage and public viewpoints.

Understanding the Opioid Epidemic. 2018. PBS.
> This documentary examines the toll of the opioid epidemic in the United States. It looks at the epidemic's impact on the individual, family, and community levels by sharing personal stories and expert viewpoints.

Warning, This Drug May Kill You. 2017. HBO Documentary Films.
> This documentary is a heartbreaking examination of the over-prescription of opioids for both major and minor health issues and how this has contributed to the opioid crisis. The impact of the crisis is shared through the personal experiences of people struggling with addiction and their loved ones.

APPENDIX B

RECOMMENDED ONLINE RESOURCES

The following is a list of online resources that provide national information on substance use and addiction. I encourage you to search for additional state and local resources.

Alcoholics Anonymous. www.aa.org.
> Alcoholics Anonymous is an international organization that supports people who have an alcohol dependency. The website contains a great deal of information, including a search tool for local AA meetings, links to literature, resources for people with an alcohol dependency and their families, and public information.

Baltimore City Health Department. You Can Stop Overdose Death. www.dontdie.org.
> This powerful website run by the Baltimore City Health Department focuses on reducing the stigma of addiction and promoting treatment, and provides information and resources that educate the public on recognizing and responding to an opioid overdose.

Center on Addiction. www.centeronaddiction.org.
> The Center on Addiction website provides resources and connections for the patients and families/caregivers of those struggling with addiction. It provides information on a variety of topics ranging from prevention to recovery.

Crisis Text Line. www.crisistextline.org/.
> This resource is not specific to addiction, but it is a great tool for anyone in a crisis. The Crisis Text Line provides free 24/7 support for anyone in the United States, Canada, and Britain. People can connect with a trained crisis counselor for any crisis at any time.

Drug Enforcement Administration. www.dea.gov.
> The DEA's website has an online fact sheet (www.dea.gov/factsheets?field_fact_sheet_category_target_id=All) that provides up-to-date information on commonly misused drugs. At the bottom of each fact page is a link to the publication *Drugs of Abuse*, which is available in PDF format and provides useful summaries of commonly misused drugs.

DualDiagnosis.org. www.dualdiagnosis.org.
> The Foundations Recovery Network runs this website, which contains a wealth of information on the relationship between substance use disorders and mental health disorders and treatment. The Foundations Recovery Network does have treatment centers, which are discussed; but regardless of whether you are interested in these services or not, the information on the site is vast and will be helpful for anyone interested in the subject of addiction and mental health.

Get Smart about Drugs: A DEA Resource for Parents, Educators, and Caregivers. www.getsmartaboutdrugs.gov.
> This site is run by the Drug Enforcement Administration and focuses on resources for educators, caregivers, and parents. There is a drop-down menu for commonly

used drugs and links to a number of free, downloadable fact sheets, posters, bookmarks, and e-books.

Just Think Twice: A Resource for Teens. www.justthinktwice.gov.
   This is another site run by the DEA and is directed toward young adults. The site not only contains an abundance of information on substance abuse and recovery, but also has many personal stories by teens who are bravely sharing their stories of addiction and recovery.

Narcotics Anonymous. www.na.org.
   Similar to Alcoholics Anonymous, Narcotics Anonymous provides meetings for individuals who are in recovery from a drug addiction. The website provides a search tool for local meetings as well as online resources and periodicals.

National Association of State Alcohol and Drug Abuse Directors (NASADAD). www.nasadad.org.
   NASADAD is a nonprofit, private organization that provides educational and scientific information to other organizations about drug and alcohol treatment programs. It works with many national and state organizations to provide information and funding on the prevention, treatment, and recovery from substance use disorders. Its published fact sheets and updates on upcoming funding and tools for national and state agencies can be very helpful when looking for information or collaborators.

National Institute on Drug Abuse. www.drugabuse.gov.
   It can feel overwhelming to keep up-to-date with current and emerging trends in drug use and addiction. The National Institute on Drug Abuse provides updated reports that anyone can subscribe to, and thereby receive e-mails when a new report is posted.

National Suicide Prevention Lifeline. www.suicidepreventionlifeline.org.
   The National Suicide Prevention Lifeline provides free and confidential 24/7 phone or online chat service for anyone in emotional distress. The website has information for families and caregivers on how to support loved ones and on targeted care for at-risk populations. The site explains what to expect when you call or chat with a counselor, which can make it less stressful for some people to reach out for help.

Operation Prevention. www.operationprevention.com.
   The DEA and Discovery Education have collaborated to educate young adults about the impact of opioids. The website contains classroom resources, videos from other young adults whose lives have been affected by addiction, and a toolkit for parents.

PillBox. https://pillbox.nlm.nih.gov.
   This pill identification website is run by the U.S. National Library of Medicine and allows people to search by name or ingredient, imprint, shape, color, or inactive ingredient. Each drug links to drug label information and general drug information.

A Prescription for Action: Local Leadership in Ending the Opioid Crisis. www.opioidaction.org.
> This website contains the report "A Prescription for Action: Local Leadership in Ending the Opioid Crisis." This report is a guide for local government officials that provides a history of the opioid crisis, why it is a crisis, and what local governments can do to combat it. I highly recommend that librarians read this report and make it available to members of local government when they are choosing to actively fight addiction in their community.

Smart Recovery. www.smartrecovery.org.
> Smart Recovery is a not-for-profit organization that helps individuals connect with free in-person and online mutual support meetings. The website also has resources for concerned family, friends, and others.

Substance Abuse and Mental Health Services Administration. www.samhsa.gov.
> A branch of the U.S. Department of Health and Human Services, the Substance Abuse and Mental Health Services Administration (SAMHSA) provides information services and research on mental health and substance use disorders to everyone. For anyone interested in learning about substance use disorders or who wants to bring informational resources into the library, this organization can be very helpful. When I reached out directly to this agency in the course of seeking professionals to speak at my library, they connected me with several individuals.

Veterans Crisis Line. www.veteranscrisisline.net.
> The Veterans Crisis Line provided by the U.S. Department of Veterans Affairs is a confidential resource available to veterans or to those who know and are concerned about a veteran. This crisis line is available twenty-four hours a day and is monitored by trained specialists in the field. It began in 2007 as a phone hotline, but the need for additional methods of contact and additional trained staff has increased dramatically, and people can now call, chat online, or text the crisis line for assistance. The Veterans Crisis Line strongly encourages veterans to reach out to it when they have mental health or substance use concerns. After speaking with someone on the line, the caller will be provided with referrals for additional services and support.

RECOMMENDED BOOKS FOR LIBRARY WORKERS

Albrecht, Steven. 2015. *Library Security: Better Communication, Safer Facilities*. Chicago: American Library Association.
> Steven Albrecht is a security specialist with a focus on workplace violence prevention. He has written many books on the topic of workplace safety, but this book is specifically written for libraries. He talks about what makes libraries so different from other locations and the importance of being aware of security issues, customer services, policies that can help librarians to address challenging behav-

iors, the common types of behaviors that library staff face, and how to respond to them. The book includes some great tools for assessing risks and collaborating with community groups.

Flaherty, Mary Grace. 2018. *Promoting Individual and Community Health at the Library.* Chicago: American Library Association.

Mary Grace Flaherty has more than twenty-five years' experience in a variety of settings, including medical research. In this short book there is a great deal of easy-to-use information on how libraries can provide health information to the public. Since many of the same groups that work with public health also support people with substance use disorders, this book can be a valuable introduction to broader ideas and concepts.

Graham, Warren. 2012. *The Black Belt Librarian: Real World Safety & Security.* Chicago: American Library Association.

This small book by Warren Graham packs a powerful punch. Graham gives twelve clear steps for libraries to adopt: establish rules and guidelines, do not make assumptions, treat everyone fairly, enforce rules consistently, be aware of the library environment, have documentation to track issues and policies to prevent those issues, train staff and volunteers, know who has the keys to various areas of the library, review policies and procedures regularly, have a security checklist, develop relationships with outside groups, and have simple emergency plans.

Nelson, Sandra S. 2003. *Creating Policies for Results: From Chaos to Clarity.* Chicago: American Library Association.

Developing policies can be stressful because of their potential importance for the public library. Policies should guide the public and staff as they access library services, and they should provide legal support when necessary. This book goes over policies in general, how to analyze current policies, and how to develop policies. There are many templates to use as a base to start policies on a wide variety of subjects.

Index

A
Adderall, 71
addiction
    caregivers and, 17
    causes of, 7–9
    as disease, 8–9
    elderly and, 16–17
    homelessness and, 14–15
    identifying, 10
    language and, 23
    library's role in fight against, 1–5
    mental health disorders and, 14
    opioid crisis and, 9
    prevention of, 3–4
    shame of, 3
    support for those affected by, 4–5
    understanding, 7–11
    veterans and, 15–16
    young adults and, 16
ADHD (attention deficit hyperactivity disorder), 71
adults, recommended books for, 91–94
aerosols, 85
AIDS, 22–23
alcohol, 74, 77–79
alcoholism, elderly and, 17
American Library Association (ALA), 1–2, 60
amobarbital, 75
amphetamines, 71–72
angel dust, 81
appearance, not relying on, 21
approving policies, 36
art programs, 41
Ativan, 76

B
barbiturates, 74–75
bathrooms, drug use in, 29
Beautiful Boy (Sheff), 4, 42
behaviors
    disruptive, 23–24
    policies for, 32–34
    problem, 15
    stigma and, 21–24
benzodiazepines, 17, 74, 76–77
Black Belt Librarian, The (Graham), 32
book displays, 45
book groups, 41
books, recommended
    for adults, 91–94
    for children, 95–96
    for library workers, 100–101
    for young adults, 94–95
Buzzed (Kuhn), 65
bystander training, 40–41

C
candlelight vigils, overdose, 53
cannabis, 84

caregivers, 17
Centers for Disease Control (CDC), 9, 26, 59
Chicken Soup for the Soul series, 43
children. *See also* young adults
   policies for, 34
   recommended books for, 95–96
cocaine, 71, 73–74
collaborative programming/services, 42, 47, 48, 51–56
Combat Methamphetamine Epidemic Act (2005), 72
communication
   with community, 3
   importance of, 19, 60
   with patrons, 10
compassion, 13
Concerta, 71
confidence, 22, 45
confidentiality, 35, 46
co-occurring disorders, 14
"Core Values of Librarianship," 1–2
crack, 71, 73–74
crystal meth, 72–73

D

date rape drugs, 77, 83
deaths due to drug overdoses, rates of, xv
deliriants, 79
delirium tremens, 79
depressants, 74–79
Desoxyn, 72–73
Deterra, 58
detox facilities, 55
Dexedrine, 71
dissociatives, 79
distress, people in, 13–19
DMT, 79
DontDie.org, 28
dopamine, 8
drug awareness programs, 40
Drug Enforcement Administration, U.S. (DEA), 9
drug use, signs of, 10, 21–22, 65–89
Dsuvia, 9

E

ecstasy (MDMA), 79, 84–85
elderly, 16–17

F

fentanyl, 27, 27*fig*, 66, 67, 69–70
films, recommended, 96–97
Food and Drug Administration (FDA), 9, 58
funding library services, 47–48

G

gases, 85
GHB (gamma-hydroxybutyric acid), 77
Good Samaritan laws, 59
Graham, Warren, 24, 32, 57–58
grieving after overdose, 18–19

H

hallucinogens, 79–85
hazardous materials, 58
"Helping Patients Cope with a Traumatic Event," 59
heroin
   about, 66, 67
   as substitute for pain medication, 15, 16
homelessness, 14–15

I

information services, 44
inhalants, 85–86

J

Jorm, Tony, 58

K

keeping up-to-date, 61
ketamine, 79, 83
Kitchener, Betty, 58
Klonopin, 76
Kuhn, Cynthia, 65

L

language
   in policies, 35–36
   relating to addiction, 23

Learn to Cope, 54
libraries
    openness of, 2, 14, 25
    outreach and marketing and, 51–56
    overdoses in, 2, 28
    policies for, 31–37
    role of in fight against
        addiction, 1–5, 63–64
    safety and security in, 25–30
    services of, 39–49
    staff training and, 57–61
Librium, 76
life-skills programming, 41–42
local organizations, 52–53
LSD (lysergic acid diethylamide), 79, 80–81

M

marijuana, 79, 84
marketing, 51–56
materials, library, 42–44
media
    outreach to, 56
    policies for, 34–35
memoirs, 43
mental health disorders, 14
Mental Health First Aid training, 58
methadone, 70
methamphetamines, 71, 72–73
mission statements, review of, 3
morphine, 66
movies, 43
music, 43

N

naloxone, 2, 27–28, 59
NaloxoneNow, 28
Narcan administration training, 41
narcotics, 65–70
National Academy of Engineering, 9
National Academy of Medicine, 9
National Academy of Science, 9
National Association of Social Workers, 47
National Council on Alcoholism and Drug Dependence, 17
National Institute on Drug Abuse, 8, 27, 61

National Library of Medicine, U.S., 60
National Recovery Month, 53
National Survey on Drug Use and Health, 14
Network for Public Health Law, 59
neurotransmitters, 8
nitrites, 85

O

off-site training, 59–60
online resources, recommended, 97–100
online training, 60
opiates and opioids, signs of use of, 65–70
opioid crisis, 9
Opioid Overdose Prevention Toolkit, 59
opium, 66
outreach, 51–56
overdoses
    candlelight vigils for, 53
    drugs involved in, 26*fig*
    from fentanyl, 27*fig*
    grieving after, 18–19
    in libraries, 2, 28
    preparedness for, xv
    preventing/prevention training and, 26–28, 59
    statistics on, 26
oxycodone, 66, 68–69
OxyContin, 9, 66, 68–69

P

patrons in crisis, working with, 2–3
PCP (phencyclidine), 79, 81–83
peer navigators, 47
pentobarbital, 75
Percocet, 68–69
Percodan, 68–69
person-first language, 23
peyote, 79
phenobarbital, 75
physiological causes of addiction, 8–9
police
    discussing library policies with, 36
    when to involve, 34
policies, library, 31–37
Preisler, Steve, 72

prescription drug drop boxes, 58
prescription pain medication,
    overprescribing of, 9
privacy, 35
problem behaviors, 15
programming, 39–42
psilocybin/psilocybin mushrooms, 79, 81
psychedelics, 79–85
psychological causes of addiction, 8
PubMed website, 7

R
radical transparency, 35
readers' advisory services, 44–46
recommended reading guides, 45–46
recovery high schools, 55
rehabilitation centers
    circulating materials to residents of, 44
    outreach to, 55
resource guides, 44–46, 53, 60
respect, 22–23
reviewing policies, 36
Ritalin, 71
rohypnol, 77
role-playing, 37
Roxicodone, 68–69

S
safety and security, 25–30, 34
secobarbital, 75
Secrets of Methamphetamine Manufacture, The (Preisler), 72
senior citizens, 16–17
serotonin, 79
sharp and hazardous materials, 58
sharps containers, 29, 58
Sheff, David, 4, 42
short stories, 43
Shulgin, Alexander, 84
sleeping in library, 33
social causes of addiction, 8
social media
    outreach and, 56
    policies for, 34–35
social responsibility, 1–2

social services, 46–47
social stigma, 3
social workers as library staff, 47
space, sharing of, 52
speaking events, 52
speed, 72–73
staff training, 57–61
starfish parable, 63–64
Stevens, Calvin, 83
stigma, 21–24
stimulants, 70–74
Substance Abuse and Mental Health
    Services Administration, 59
sudden sniffing death syndrome (SSDS),
    85–86
suicide rates among veterans, 15

T
television programs, recommended, 96–97
training
    creating program for, 60
    policy, 36–37
    staff, 57–61
traumatic events, coping with, 59

U
U.S. Drug Enforcement Administration
    (DEA), 9
U.S. National Library of Medicine, 60

V
Valium, 76
veterans, 15–16
Veterans Affairs facilities, 15–16
violence, 25
volatile solvents, 85

W
WebJunction, 61
withdrawal, as motivator for drug use, 10
writing policies, 35–36

X
Xanax, 76
Xtampza ER, 68–69

Y
yoga programs, 41
young adults. *See also* children
    addiction and, 16
    outreach to, 55
    recommended books for, 94–95

www.ingramcontent.com/pod-product-compliance
Lightning Source LLC
Chambersburg PA
CBHW061418300426
44114CB00015B/1980